FOUR FABULOUS FACES

Ho...
himself ap...
and recordi...
for th...
in...

In April,
New York City
postwar supper c...
In July, he began singing on ...
own radio show. A Broadway music
followed quickly and then Hollywood bec...
For the next two decades, films, TV, record
comp... writing,

FOUR FABULOUS FACES

SWANSON

GARBO

CRAWFORD

DIETRICH

LARRY CARR

GALAHAD BOOKS · NEW YORK CITY

This edition of FOUR FABULOUS FACES published by Galahad
Books, a subsidiary of A & W Promotional Book Corp., by per-
mission of Arlington House.

Library of Congress Catalog Card No.: 73-79810

ISBN: 0-88365-044-4

MANUFACTURED IN THE UNITED STATES OF AMERICA

ACKNOWLEDGMENTS

Inestimable gratitude and thanks are due a great many people who generously contributed to this book; some offered material, anecdotes and photographs, others gave their time and encouragement. Without the assistance of all of them, it would have been impossible to complete this project.

I am grateful to Ron Alexander, Larry Ashmead, Anita Louise Berger, Harold Berkin, Jane Brent, Eulalia Chapin, Milly Considine, Sanford Dody, Joan Dunham, Millie Emory, Sherman Emory, William K. Everson, Evelyn Fiore, Joe Franklin, Ron Galella, Ermina Stimson Goble, Milton Goldman, Ernest V. Heyn, Maurice Johnson, Herbert Jonas, Leon Kellman, Fred Koch, Don Koll, Abril Lamarque, Joseph Longo, Bud McCreery, Bob Miller, Marion Morgan, Ann Pinchot, Dale Phillips, Frankie McKee Robins, Sue Salter, Robert P. Smith, L. Arnold Weissberger, and Jerome Zerbe for their assistance and encouragement.

I owe incalculable gratitude to Marcus Blechman who, when I started working on this book, generously gave me so many photographs. Special thanks are due the other master photographers for the use of their superb portraits: Richard Avedon, Cecil Beaton, Edward Carroll, Milton Greene, Horst P. Horst, Irving Penn, and John Rawlings. I am indebted to them all and to Bernard Perlin for the portraits by George Platt Lynes.

Special thanks go to the following people whose contribution of photographs and material from their private collections made possible this rare ensemble: Eugene Burde, Homer Dickens, Frank Driggs, Warren Harris, William Kenley, Hilary Knight, Jerry Lang, Dion McGregor, William Pratt, Fred Romary, Romano Tozzi, Avery Willard, and Peter Windsor.

During my research, I was helped immeasurably by Paul Myers and the staff of the Lincoln Center theater collection; by Eve Bayne, chief librarian of Dell Publications; Vivian Sinise Poppenberg, Jack Podell, Patricia DeJager and the staff of MacFadden-Bartell Publications; Mrs. Esther Ford Robinson of Street and Smith; Mary Mills and staff of Fawcett Publications; the staff of *Movie Star News* and by photographs from *H.D.* collection.

I must thank George Frazier for introducing me to Martin Gross and Arlington House, and I am beholden to Marty, my editor, for his enthusiastic encouragement and understanding. To Bob Cato and Norman Seeff, I must give unstinted praise and thanks for the extraordinary and sensitively beautful book they have helped create. Grateful acknowledgment is made to Paul H. Bonner of Condé Nast for his gracious and generous help in obtaining photographs and material that appeared in *Vanity Fair, Vogue* and *Glamour;* to Ralph Daigh of Fawcett Publications and to Fred Klein and Mark J. Greenberg of MacFadden-Bartell for permission to reproduce the magazine covers in the color section of this book; and to Sam Pearce and Melvin Park of the Museum of the City of New York for their assistance.

Last but not at all least, my affectionate thanks to Adela Rogers St. Johns for her warm introduction to *Four Fabulous Faces,* and my sincere appreciation to Miss Gloria Swanson and her secretary, Miss Gladys Griffith, for their help in securing photographs that enhance this book. Thanks go to the studios of Warner Brothers, Paramount, Columbia, M-G-M, 20th-Century-Fox, and United Artists, and to Associated Press and INS. My indebtedness to all the above and to any others whom I may have inadvertently overlooked is much too voluminous to be thoroughly documented, but I do tender recognition to everyone with all possible gratitude and appreciation.

CONTENTS

I

INTRODUCTION
by Adela Rogers St. Johns

A return to a glamorous past when times in art often seem to speak another language, scientific, mediocre, ugly and grim, is the secret yearning of many hearts. When Romance has vanished in favor of so-called Realism—as though the Rose were not as real as the Manure—I find even the Young peering back to see what it was like *then.* With Hollywood giving off the same aura as Pompeii, with the big studios no longer in existence, with absurd costs and considerable lack of talent sending the younger producers and stars in all directions for new fields, we still have a desire to know what it was *like* then. *Then—* in the old days of making *Gone with the Wind,* the old days of Jack Gilbert and Garbo, of Humphrey Bogart and Ingrid Bergman at their peak, of Bette Davis bringing Elizabeth the Great to *life* in one of her never-equaled performances, of *The* Movie Star, Gloria Swanson wedding the first Title, of Marlene Dietrich becoming—actually—a star overnight in a picture called *The Blue Angel,* of Joan Crawford sweeping all before her from *Our Modern Maidens* to *Mildred Pierce.*
These I have let flow from this battered typewriter without second thought, for they are things I remember with love, with, I hope, a kind of Loyalty, and certainly with that tragically abused word Nostalgia—and it is tragically abused because even with the help of *Roget's Thesaurus* I can think of no other. I want to see again what I once knew so well—the glamorous romantic pioneer days of The Movies. The days when indeed A Movie Star was the ONLY all-encompassing star except maybe Babe Ruth. When Lon Chaney's death stopped the telephone company's switchboards for hours with weeping prayers and disbelief. When Tom Mix created the Western. When The Talkies Came it was to us rather like Sherman marching through Georgia. And the little old California town, streets lined with orange trees and peppers and adobe mansions, was the Capital of the Film Art and Industry.

I want to see, think about, remember all this and much more again. I find as I travel about talking in colleges and high schools and to young women's clubs and young men's organizations they are hotly curious about that age, that place, that cast of characters.
Larry Carr was there.
With a tuned ear and a trained eye, he lived as part of this, successfully and fully, behind the scenes and as entertainer, musician, singer, piano player in the Duchin class, actor, producer and often writer, in front of the camera and the backdrops.
From time to time when we were neighbors for periods in New York we used to "visit" back in these Good Old Days. We used to talk about the Stars that were then, the scandals that nearly—and sometimes wholly—destroyed them, the glorious and philanthropic things they did, the rebellious YOUTH that pervaded it all. For the stars then were ALL young. We were all pioneers. Things happened to us. And I found Larry one of my favorite companions in sessions of true Reminiscence. Oh, he was there all right—and his memories are clear, his perspective sympathetic and emotional and truthful.
Out of those memories and perhaps partly as a result of those talks, he has brought some of them into a book called *Four Fabulous Faces*—and FABULOUS they are. How can Joan Crawford, Greta Garbo, Gloria Swanson and Marlene Dietrich be otherwise?
You will take a real tour of the glamorous, romantic, violent, and inspired days that MADE The Movies.
I don't say they were necessarily better—or worse—or bigger or smaller—though to me it seems we've flattened out a good deal. But that they were different and much, much, much more filled with love, laughter, and tears—that they were different—I do say.
And as you read Larry Carr, I'm pretty sure you'll say so too.

This book is a pictorial
history of four women who possess in a supreme
measure a glitter, a magnetism, a bewitching sorcery
that appeal to *men* and *women* to a degree seldom,
if ever, matched in our time. Glamour is defined as
"alluring charm or fascination, often based on illusion,
that transforms or glorifies a person or thing." It is my
hope that *all* generations will find in this book not only
nostalgia for a glamour that is practically non-existent
today, but also a study in depth of four faces that had
and still have glamour in such abundance.
Their names are synonymous with glamour. Each, in her
own way, still carries its aura with her. To me, they are
the most charismatic of all of this century's beautiful
women who have helped millions of people fantasize
erotic adventures denied them in real life. For nearly
five decades, they have created illusion and beauty
and excitement.
The 70s are here now and it's all quite different from
the decades when these four faces reigned so gloriously.
It's real, it's earnest, it's honest. It's also brutal, defiant,
and ugly. Daydreams are difficult in an era that seems
to glorify the average, the homely, the inelegant. Gauche
is considered chic, clumsy is graceful, the unpre-
possessing regarded as "neat." Yet an older generation
who *know* this is not true, and a younger one who
somehow intuitively feel it, no matter how standards of
beauty have changed, will still appreciate authenticity
when it can be found. And here *is* authentic glamour,
beauty and escapism.
The concept for this book began in 1964 when I was
producing a series of albums for Columbia and Epic
Records, devoted to the music of the 20s and 30s.
Besides evaluating and choosing the musical selections,
I also wrote the liner-notes and supplied the photographs that adorned the covers and booklets in the
albums, all of which required a hell of a lot of research
and interviews. Searching through hundreds of books
and periodicals devoted to those earlier decades, I
began to be aware, very slowly at first and then with
increasing frequency, of several items of interest that
eventually led to the compilation and writing of this book.
Libraries and publishing companies had kindly allowed
me access to their files and, as I went through bound
copies of magazines year by year, I was amazed to see
how early in their careers a number of performers who
are now known for the longevity of those careers were
being written off as "fading"—or "finished," especially
the four subjects of this tome. As early as 1925, magazine articles were asking, "Can Gloria last?" and, by
1927, "Is Swanson through?" Having just seen Gloria
Swanson looking miraculously beautiful on a top TV
program the evening before, I was more than a little
amused. As I continued my research, I read a 1929
article, "Will Garbo Survive the Talkies?" during the
same period in which a festival of her films was breaking
all records at New York's Museum of Modern Art.
"Is Dietrich Through?" headlined a 1933 *Photoplay,*
which I saw while the lady in question was the sensation
of the 1968 Broadway season with her incomparable
one-woman show. Joan Crawford, still deploying her
star-emeritus status in films and on TV as spokeswoman
for Pepsi-Cola, was declared box-office poison by

theater exhibitors in the 30s and "through" a number of
times since then. Joan has just finished her 86th movie!
Then the second thing that impressed me as I pored
chronologically over masses of old magazines—*Vanity
Fair, Life, Vogue,* various screen and radio magazines
et al.—was the startling, remarkable metamorphosis of
the four faces and the tremendous influence which they
had had on both the look of other women and the
fashions of their times. During a given period, all the
models in ads, the mannequins in fashion, the girls in
illustrations for stories, would suddenly look like one of
these stars. It was a fascinating discovery for me to
follow through each decade the evolution of these four
women into great beauties and fabulous faces and I
wanted to document their lasting impression on our age
and culture. I determined to do a book in which I could
share my pleasure and excitement and viewpoint.
Then began the search for photographs that would
properly tell my story. It was a long and arduous task,
which became unbelievably expensive as I got further
into the project of securing the material that I needed.
Some people were incredibly difficult and disagreeable
to deal with while others astounded me with their kind-
ness, generosity and help. However, I was hooked—
and the more unpaid time I devoted to it, at the expense
of other work, only strengthened my determination to
persist until I could have the book I had envisioned.
So I continued, bought and borrowed over 5,000 photographs, purchased nearly 500 magazines and several
hundred books, and after five years finally compiled
the end result—this book.
Now you may ask, as others have:
Why *these* FOUR FABULOUS FACES? Why *this* choice?
Because, more than any other of their contemporaries,
these four living legends have lasted longest, endured
best and still are outstanding and shining examples of
beauty and glamour, continuing to possess those
qualities which attract and fascinate, and which command attention, enthusiasm and approbation.

Gloria Swanson, Greta Garbo, Joan Crawford and
Marlene Dietrich have been written about, talked about,
photographed and painted more often than any other
women of the 20th century. During their long careers
and public lives, all four have undergone a gradual
metamorphosis, reflecting both personal and social
change, which mirrored and helped set the style and
look of succeeding decades. They have exerted a tremendous influence on women all over the world who
copied their clothes, style and makeup. When Swanson
bobbed her hair in the early 20s, millions of women
rushed to imitate her. Remember Garbo's long bob,
Empress Eugenie hat and her famous slouch? And
Crawford's enormous mouth and eyes, broad shoulders
and "Letty Lynton" dress? And Dietrich's famous slacks
and mannish apparel, her cock feathers and boas, fish-
tail skirts and flesh-like gowns? They are part of our
fashion heritage.
It all began after World War I, when a most dramatic
change in women's appearance took place, one that
was the most startling and far-reaching in the entire
history of beauty: the voluptuous, full-bosomed woman
who had always intrigued men in previous centuries was

supplanted by the slim boyish flapper. Women's foreheads, which for generations had been hidden under elaborate hair designs and been swathed in turbans or immersed in enormous, towering hats, emerged until they were completely exposed. Smoothly cropped heads with a boyish bob set off a new look in faces, with the eyes and mouth accentuated in a novel and staggeringly theatrical fashion. Pretty faces gave way to striking ones, smooth and fresh, with hair very short and sleekly shingled to expose the ears.

It was during this period that Gloria Swanson rose to stardom and influence. From photographs taken throughout the past fifty years, one can see her face evolve and develop. Miss Swanson began her recreation back in the early 20s, when, after serving a brief apprenticeship with Mack Sennett, she went to work for Cecil B. DeMille in his marital soap operas. He made a clothes horse out of her, gowned her elaborately and flamboyantly, piled her hair in artificial, perilous heights on her head. The fans loved it, and the opulent films in which he starred her attracted women to movie theaters as those of no other actress. Swanson's shrewd intelligence told her that she really looked neither smart nor chic.

So, when she went to New York in 1923 to make a film and observed the trim, sleek women there, she dispensed with her former artifice, dropped the DeMille posturing, and simplified her clothes and makeup. The results made her look not only much younger, but infinitely more attractive, and the "new Swanson" of The Humming Bird and Manhandled drew a larger, more discerning box-office following.

In 1925, she went to Paris to film Madame Sans Gene, where she met and married the Marquis de la Falaise de la Coudraye. With a French title, Parisian clothes and overwhelming public interest and curiosity, she returned to America to be given an unprecedented welcome home.

By this time, she was the number-one box-office attraction—having wrested the cinema crown away from Mary Pickford, who till then had shared with Douglas Fairbanks this exalted position. Swanson became the acknowledged queen of Hollywood; everything she did was news; everything she wore was copied. An awed Hollywood that remembered her "when" saw a radiantly recreated Swanson who contributed immensely to a new look for women, who changed the concept of beauty from one of doll-like pastel prettiness of sugar-spun perfection to one of intelligence, emphasizing bone structure, strong features and a smooth, clean line of individuality. By sheer force of personality and mind, she turned her non-conforming features to advantage by accentuating their unusual, distinctive points: the large almond-shaped eyes, the tilting nose, the dazzling square smile with the Chiclet teeth, set in a face that achieved beauty in its own way, quite unlike anyone else before or since.

Her grooming, sparkle and radiant style became (and have continued to be) the unforgettable epitome of elegance and feminine enchantment. Women everywhere, including her screen contemporaries—Aileen Pringle, Fay Wray, Lupe Velez, Pauline Stark, and the young up-and-coming Joan Crawford, among others—all tried on the Swanson look. But there was—and is—only one Swanson!

After 1925, further peaks lay ahead—more triumphs and her Academy Award nominations for Sadie Thompson, The Trespasser, and Sunset Boulevard; but there were also the valleys of those grim years when she was a "has-been" out of public favor. Through it all, Swanson the woman, Swanson the fabulous face, has endured,

remaining a wondrous example of what drive, discipline and intelligence can achieve.

Then came Garbo. Introduced to American audiences in 1926, she became the next great screen beauty of worldwide impact. Her two previous European films, which had a limited showing in this country, only hinted at the enigmatic magic that was so to intrigue, baffle and captivate her audience. At first, Garbo was reminiscent of several other stars of the day: at this period, pictures of her and of Crawford and Dietrich, too, show the short, bobbed hair, unruly and frizzled, that was prevalent in the mid-20s. Garbo's famous shoulder-length bob, burnished and smoothly brushed, was to come later in 1928, by which time her rapid metamorphosis into an enchantingly unique type had begun to alter the existing standards of beauty.

Her chiseled, sensitive features, luminous eyes framed with extraordinarily long lashes, heavily darkened and accentuated for the camera, plus the wide, generous mouth with its petulant pout, the straight nose and the exquisitely shaped head, held high on the tall, slender body with its famous slouch, created a striking contrast to the prevailing mode. Garbo was as different as possible from Swanson who, in turn, had been such a change from Mary Pickford and everyone else before her. Garbo was tall, Swanson was small; Garbo was languid, Swanson was energetic; Garbo was foreign, Swanson was American.

The Garbo whom Hollywood created bore no resemblance to the shy, gauche young woman who arrived in New York in 1925 from Sweden, wearing an ill-fitting checked suit which did little for her. Nor did her frizzed hair, her shoes which were run down at the heels, or her stockings, one of which had a well-defined run, help her appearance. She spoke no English, only Swedish and a smattering of German. After spending a lonely, hot summer in New York while M-G-M officials tried to decide what to do with this foreigner who fitted no then-known conception of screen heroines, she was ready to give up and return home. But Arnold Genthe, the distinguished photographer, took some portraits of her that persuaded the studio to give her a chance in Hollywood. Arriving there, she was met by a lone photographer. "Where would you like to live while you're here?" she was asked through an interpreter. Modestly, slowly, she gave the reply that became a classic among the Garbo legends.

"I think," she said, "I like private room with nice family—one which will not cost too much." In the ensuing years, the world was to become much better acquainted with the Garbo frugality.

Within the next year, there were interesting changes and developments as she became more familiar with the film colony and its habits. She was arrested for speeding in her new (secondhand) green car. She acquired a maid (a requisite for any film star!) and an increasing sense of her importance in pictures, turning a deaf ear to anyone and anything she did not like.

She learned English slowly, for she was not particularly anxious to learn it, nor did silent films require it.

Standing beneath a fig tree on the M-G-M lot one day not long after she arrived, she ate some of the fruit, disregarding a sign which warned that it must not be touched. A studio cop came running up. "You mustn't pull them figs!" he shouted. "Whatsa matter witcha? Can'cha read?" Garbo eyed him coldly, tossed away the stem, and gave him a large part of her stock American vocabulary in reply. "Beat it!" she replied, as she strolled away. No one knew where she learned the two words.

By 1930, Garbo was the biggest female attraction in

Hollywood. She had such a sweeping effect on women everywhere that it became *de rigueur* for every young woman to wear the shoulder-length bob and slouch-hat that were synonymous with her. Garboites filled cinema theaters during her career and continue to do so today whenever her films are shown. She remains a legend, intriguing and unfathomable, and the reasons for this are examined and illustrated in the chapter devoted to her.

Following Garbo, the next great impact on the public—and on women's fashions—was Joan Crawford, my third Fabulous Face. In 1925, the same year that Garbo arrived from Sweden, a plump, pretty but commonplace Joan Crawford came from the Broadway chorus to Hollywood.

She spent the next five years experimenting with her looks and so changing them that the result was a variety of faces. Sometimes, she was hardly recognizable from one film to the next. For a while she resembled a young Pauline Frederick, then switched to emulating Gloria Swanson until she fell under the Garbo influence. She dieted her chubby figure to a slender one, made her large eyes even more enormous with heavy makeup, painted her lips every shape and size, dyed her hair a range of colors, until finally, by 1932, she was transformed into the strong and distinctive personality that has been so easily recognizable for the past four decades. Although she has continued to alter subtly her appearance through the years as fashions changed, she has always retained the basic "Joan Crawford" look of the thirties. Her huge following has remained steadfastly loyal in a business where the public is famous for its "off with the old, on with the new" attitude, making her perennial popularity a tribute to the determination and hard work that changed a gauche chorus girl into a movie queen of beauty, personality and radiance. In the past few years she has become a well-known business woman, combining this and her acting career with rare success.

In their book, *The Movies*, Arthur Mayer and Richard Griffith (of the Museum of Modern Art film library), in the chapter "The Indestructibles," which lists Gable, Bogart, Tracy, Dietrich, Hepburn, Chaplin, Cary Grant, etc., name Crawford "the most Durable Dame of Them All." They point out that "professional longevity would seem to be the most objective test of this, and by that yardstick Joan Crawford wins hands down."

Actually, Swanson's career began ten years earlier than Crawford's, but she has not remained so active in films as has Crawford. Dietrich's career started in Germany about the same time as Crawford's but she didn't reach stardom until 1931, two years later than Joan. Certainly, all three have endured by their amazing survival value, their inventiveness and adaptability.

The Fourth Fabulous Face is Marlene Dietrich, who, like the other three, is truly a "living legend." Now Mr. Webster defines a legend as "a romantic story; myth, fable…an authentic narrative handed down by tradition. "Dietrich and the many versions of her life story have gradually been incorporated into a legend. Her long and varied career, her great beauty, her romances and friendships with writers, generals, baseball players, and statesmen have all contributed to it.

It was in 1930 that she burst upon the scene and ignited the world's admiration in *The Blue Angel*, playing the part of a sultry nightclub singer whose "face and body drove men mad!" It was an unforgettable performance. Today, at an age acknowledged to be in the late sixties, and four times a grandmother, Dietrich is still playing the same role on the stages of the world. She is one of the greatest nightclub and theater acts of our time, still lovely, slim and incredibly glamorous. The only difference now is that her face and body are much more likely to drive *women* mad because of her miraculous youthfulness. They go to see the legend, to see if it's all true and to hope that, somehow, they can achieve the same thing, that a little of her youthfulness might rub off on them.

Wherever she appears, be it Las Vegas, London, Paris, New York, South America, Germany, Israel or Australia, her impact is the same, and her audiences, some of which come to be shown, *are* shown—and conquered! The caressing voice and matchless legs are incorporated into a highly disciplined and versatile act, which presents Marlene in glamorous furs and clinging gowns. So the Dietrich name and the Dietrich personality remain as potent as ever, fed by new and youthful admirers who are discovering her for the first time and by the faithful followers of many years.

As in the case of Garbo, the young Dietrich starting in German films in the late 20s was decidedly different from the woman to become world-renowned. At that time she showed few of the unique qualities which were subsequently to distinguish her. Both she and Garbo had faces too heavy for American tastes and were then so unremarkable that even today it is difficult to detect in their European films much evidence of the qualities that were to contribute to their later image. Dietrich, too, had to slim down; new grooming, makeup and (most importantly) lighting produced results that were truly astonishing. Although Dietrich's photographic resemblance to Garbo was at first stressed in her films and photographs, her natural humor and vitality were so readily apparent that she became a personality completely her own. Her newly discovered beauty was displayed for awhile in films that were considered too static and in which her loveliness was overemphasized to the detriment of her acting. However, she re-emerged in *Destry Rides Again* (1939) as a performer of remarkable energy, with her sense of humor and warm empathy again properly displayed to re-establish a career that has since persisted as a phenomenon in films and nightclubs all over the world. Her lengthy war record in performing for the Allied troops further enhanced her legend, and to this day she remains an erotic delight to the eye and ear, a performer whose appearances break box-office records everywhere.

Thus all four faces follow a pattern: All started with little hint of greatness, evolving from small beginnings. All worked hard and persevered to build careers that took them to the top as actresses and as beauties. And all have left their marks as great beauties, stars and living legends on our society and culture.

Each decade has seen them photographed by the most gifted artists of the day, and these photographs have contributed to the look of their time. All are still known the world over for the longevity of their glamour, beauty, intelligence and influence, their names synonymous with fashion, luxury and glamour. They are a ringing message of hope for those who are in search of these attributes.

Therefore, it seems to me that these Four Women are unique and the most extraordinary of all the Hollywood women. Ineffably glamorous—they have remained stars supreme.

Now turn the pages and watch the evolution and metamorphosis of Four Fabulous Faces.

How do you describe a cyclone—a whirlwind of past experiences and future expectations? Gloria Swanson's life has been a fairy tale that any self-respecting writer would blush to invent: a movie extra in Chicago at 15, a Mack Sennett comedienne in Hollywod at 17, the wife of actor Wallace Beery at 18, a full-fledged movie star at 21, a Marquise and the greatest film attraction in the world at 26, and then, suddenly, a "has-been" at 33. By that time she had discarded four husbands, had three children, made over a million dollars and spent every cent of it.

Gloria Swanson has a magnificent capacity for survival, for turning defeat into victory. A few people are lucky enough sometimes to make *one* comeback after sliding from the top: she has made five! She was seventy-one on March 27, 1970, and she has remained the epitome of the word "star" in its fullest sense.

Always a pioneering spirit, she was the first top star to have a baby. She not only admitted it, at a time when having a child was deeply discouraged and frowned upon, but gloried in it and made motherhood for stars fashionable.

A distinct, definite personality, she is attracted by other definite personalities and by people with ideas. A visit with her guarantees rapid-fire discussions that range through a multitude of subjects from philosophy to the latest invention.

She possesses the grace, savoir faire and cosmopolitan sophistication acquired by one who has enjoyed the stimulation of living in Biarritz, Paris, London and Portugal. She has kept the same apartment in New York for thirty years but spends much of her time living elsewhere.

In late 1969, she returned from Portugal, where she has spent most of the past two years, to attend the wedding in California of her granddaughter.

Whatever the future may hold for her, she eagerly looks forward to it, and her deep interest in living continues unabated. She defies classification.

GLORIA SWANSON

7

Greta Garbo has not made
a motion picture since 1941, and it is highly unlikely that
she will ever make another. Of the Four Faces in this book,
her career, consisting of just 15 brief years, was the
shortest—yet her place both in screen history and in the
annals of the 20th century is unique and secure. So extraordinarily brilliant was that career that there can never be
anything like it again. And so deeply etched on the public
consciousness is that Fabulous Face that she remains
unduplicable as a Beauty, Actress and Personality.
For she had a conception of performance and a rare
personal quality, combining the spiritual and the sensual,
that were a paradox of precision and fantasy. Her amalgam
of vigorous voluptuousness and tender dignity made her
an inimitable creature of dreams and flesh.
Some of her films, when seen today, seem mediocre and
run-of-the-mill in themselves; yet they have achieved the
status of classics due solely to her presence in them. One
must be grateful that, through the magic of motion pictures
and photography, her beauty and her acting throughout
her entire career can still be seen, preserved by the camera
for generation after generation to study and savor.
Hers has been called "The Face of this Century." Certainly
she is one of the world's foremost legendary beauties, and
the unmatched compilation of photographs in this book
gives ample evidence of this truth. I think I may securely
say that it is the most thorough chronological study ever
published of her face. Due to the fact that Garbo posed for
only a limited amount of photographs at the studio during
her career (and these were nearly always in conjunction
with her current film) and almost none outside, the entire
sum of Garbo photographs in existence is consequently
very limited. (The span of photographs for the other three
Faces covers a period of nearly 50 years.)
Characterized by Alice B. Toklas as "Mademoiselle
Hamlet," she lives, as always, a singularly private life today,
which continues to tantalize and intrigue her public as
much as her enigmatic beauty and personality do. And
Garbo, the classic star, lives on in her camera image—a
legend and a myth.

GRETA GARBO

Joan Crawford has just

recently finished her 86th motion picture: she remains one of the industry's all-time greatest stars. In 45 years of screen performances, she has progressed from a *Dancing Daughter* and *Modern Maiden* to a *Blushing Bride*: she has advanced from a *Gorgeous Hussy* and a *Woman's Face* to *Mildred Pierce*, from chopping up people with dialogue in *Harriet Craig* and *Baby Jane* to the outright mayhem of axes and hammers in *Strait Jacket* and *I Saw What You Did*. In her current film, *Trog*, playing a lady scientist, she is content with taming a prehistoric man-ape. For the past decade, she has been not only an actress but a business woman as well, handling a huge public relations job that keeps her traveling, on the average, 200,000 miles a year. She's a far cry from the Broadway chorus girl who came to Hollywood in 1925 to try her luck in pictures, and it's difficult to believe that she is the same person.

But how much has she *actually* changed?

In an article written for *Vanity Fair* in July 1930, her then husband, Douglas Fairbanks, Jr., wrote, "She has the most remarkable power of concentration of anyone I have ever known. Under any circumstances this tremendous faculty is at her very fingertips. She is consumed with an overwhelming ambition.

"She is always prepared for any emergency. She has a great capacity for study. If she feels that she is not up to standard in a certain line she will go to any extreme to master it.

"She is not easily influenced and must be thoroughly convinced before she will waver in her opinion on any point. She must always feel herself moving forward, and when anything tends to arrest that progress she sulks mentally. She will stand by a belief with Trojan ferocity. She has temperament without being temperamental. She demands the things to which she knows she has the right, and will ask for no more until she knows with all sincerity she is worthy of it. This is particularly true in her professional life.

"She takes a great interest in clothes and all things feminine yet has the analytical mind of a man. She is an excellent business woman but a poor trader. She is intolerant of people's weaknesses. If someone does her a wrong she is slow in forgetting it but when she does there is no doubt of her attitude. She is embarrassingly honest in her opinions....She is forever devising new ways to fix her hair. She loves to cook...is thoughtful to a point of extravagance ...is sensitive about her lower teeth being crooked....

She takes a pardonable pride in the strides that she has made in her chosen field yet she is never satisfied with her work. Jealousy is not in her makeup, but she resents those who have become successful without serving the same trying apprenticeship that she herself experienced. She has a tendency to dramatize any anecdote which she may relate. Music affects her emotionally. She is sentimental to an extreme degree. She is a ten-year-old girl who has put on her mother's dress—and has done it convincingly."

Forty years later, this seems an accurate and penetrating character sketch of a woman "consumed with an overwhelming ambition," who "must always feel herself moving forward," who still will "demand the things to which she knows she has the right." She is still a woman who "takes a great interest in clothes...loves to cook...resents those who have become successful without serving [her] same trying apprenticeship."

Mr. Fairbanks wrote a most penetrating, perceptive pen portrait.

JOAN CRAWFORD

11

The Dietrich image, created essentially by the phantasmagoria of her beauty in films of the 30s and 40s, has become part of the mythology of our times. She has nurtured and kept it in existence by carefully calculated appearances in a few other films, by her one-woman show which she has played all over the world, and by her own innate sense of publicity and self-display.

Utilizing her arsenal of allure, she first stormed the senses and mesmerized her audiences as "the reigning beauty of the screen" (which is how Paramount advertised her in the 30s), then matured into an actress and performer of international repute. Her old friend Maurice Chevalier said, "Marlene Dietrich had the guts that Greta Garbo never had in continuing her career. Marlene has a lot of guts and it's surprising to find that in one so feminine" (Earl Wilson, *New York Post,* July 29, 1967).

Like Swanson, she is intensely interested in everything and extremely knowledgeable about art, literature, fashion, diet and medicine. Tallulah Bankhead once said, "If I were sick and couldn't get Florence Nightingale, I'd get Marlene."

To exhaust her is apparently impossible: it is she who exhausts others, and this has been true through the years from director Josef Von Sternberg, who knew how to use her boundless ability for hard work, to those who have come into contact with the woman who is star, producer and director of *Marlene Dietrich,* a Nine O'Clock Theatre Production. Co-workers and technicians view with awe her knowledge of the tools of her trade, camera, lights, sound, costumes and publicity. She is the only Hollywood star who was ever elected an honorary member of Local 706, the studio makeup and hairdressers union.

She remains the Boadicea of stage performers with her sardonic sexuality and sublime air of lethal tranquility heating up theaters all over the world.

MARLENE DIETRICH

IV

their growing pains right out in public for the world to see, saying what they pleased, dressing as they pleased, and living as they pleased. Their homes were bougainvillea-covered bungalows and plaster palaces, with the film titans ensconced lavishly on Whitley Avenue or "north of the Boulevard." When their wallets and imagination ran rampant, the results were often awe-inspiring. Beverly Hills was still a long distance from Hollywood, and at the time that Swanson bought a twenty-four-room house there in 1920, which had been built by razor magnate King Gillette, she was one of the very first actors to invade its dignified atmosphere. Ingrown as Hollywood was during this embryonic period, its pictures quickly enthralled the U.S. public and then the world; for *pantomime* was a universal language, immediately understood by everyone, that films gradually began to elevate to an art form despite the uninhibited acting and crude plots. Overemphasized were clothes, sets, acting styles and techniques, reflecting the absence of subtlety which characterized not only Hollywood but the whole era—those mad, whirlwind years that followed World War I.

Gloria Swanson (an overdressed odalisque in the DeMille extravanganzas) was only a part of the youthful flamboyancy of this turbulent decade in which the people making movies grew incredibly rich in an impossibly short time.

Hollywood could not yet compete with New York, London or Paris, which catered to a mature, sophisticated but limited audience. It was mass-producing films that told fairy tales which in those innocent days were easily understood in any country by a worldwide audience of millions. It supplied in generous helpings any and every emotion to this new audience that could now afford the price of a ticket to see the movies it so eagerly craved.

As Hollywood matured, it attracted people with imagination and inventiveness, so the naiveté and gaucherie that had characterized its early films began to fade out. Stories grew bolder as pictures got longer: characterizations ripened into believable people so that audiences were able to identify with certain players. They began demanding to see more of the personalities whom they had grown to know and love, with the result that, despite all efforts of the picture makers to keep control of the situation, the public created its own stars. Each personality was different—individual—and there was no mistaking one for the other. There was only one Pickford, one Fairbanks, one Chaplin, one Swanson, one Pearl White, and their imitators never lasted very long. Wallace Reid, Richard Barthelmess, Lon Chaney, Wallace Beery and Francis X. Bushman were great favorites of the women while the men responded to the charms of Norma and Constance Talmadge, Mae Murray, Pola Negri, Corinne Griffith, Alice Joyce and Bebe Daniels.

Gloria Swanson was originally a product of Hollywood, who was refined by New York, London and Paris. She arrived in California from Chicago at 17, an age at which most girls were in high school, and spent the next few years learning and developing her craft in a small town—friendly, naive and ambitious—that was almost as young as she was, where everybody knew everybody in an atmosphere of casual democracy.

Like most other small towns, there were no traditions in Hollywood—still in the making were the future first families and proud privileged aristocracy. The second and third generation DeMilles, Goldwyns, Fairbanks, Chaplins *et al.,* were yet to come. Then, it was juvenile, crude and as precocious as a spoiled child. But the film colony also was friendly, ambitious and enthusiastic. For this was the era of hope, courage and invention, and the films that it produced for an eager public reflected these characteristics. As yet, there was no interference or guidance from the bankers and businessmen from the East. One stood on his own, doing his thing as he saw fit, with an abundance of originality and high spirits.

The climate was sunny, creating a happy, relaxed atmosphere conducive to hard work and to playful holidays. Most of the film colony had migrated from the studios of New York City and Chicago, so Hollywood's orange and eucalyptus groves, palm trees, orchards, and flower and vegetable gardens were a refreshing change from the cold rains and slushy snows that they had left. In this free and uninhibited climate they had

In every field, there were young giants. Among the directors D. W. Griffith was creating celluloid history with new techniques like the *closeup* and *fadeout*, while he modified the broad stage style of acting into a more restrained one for the camera. A great innovator, Griffith guided the careers of Lillian and Dorothy Gish, Mae Marsh, Bobby Harron, Henry B. Walthall and Blanche Sweet. Also creating important pictures were William and Cecil B. DeMille, Henry King, Marshall Neilan, Hal Roach, Erich Von Stroheim, Rex Ingram, James Cruze and Maurice FitzMaurice.

Mack Sennett led the comedy parade in films featuring his famous cops and such bathing beauties as Gloria Swanson, Bebe Daniels, Phyllis Haver and Marie Provost. From him came the comedy "chase" with the crazy automobiles and trolley cars, the cops and robbers, and such diverse talents as Charlie Chaplin, Mabel Normand, Harold Lloyd, Fatty Arbuckle, Mack Swain, Chester Conklin, Raymond Griffith, Ford Sterling, Louise Fazenda and Marie Dressler.

William S. Hart, Buck Jones and, especially, Tom Mix fashioned the cowboy, forging a golden link to Gary Cooper, John Wayne and the many others who were to follow. They built a universal audience for the western which has proved to be the most enduring and copied of all Hollywood screen genera.

Nepotism began to develop as producers, directors and stars employed their relatives in ever-increasing numbers. The Laemmles, Zukors, Mayers, Schencks, Selznicks and Goldwyns originated the dynasties destined to run Hollywood for many years. Keaton, Fairbanks, Lloyd and Chaplin all had their fathers and brothers helping them, while famous "movie mothers" included Charlotte Pickford, Peg Talmadge, Phyllis Daniels, Mrs. Gish and Mrs. Minter, to name only a few of the matriarchy.

Beautiful girls poured into Hollywood, all sizes and shapes, with complexions and hair of every color. Some were imported and some just came but all were attracted by the prospect of quick film fame. Among those who made it were Alice Joyce, Lois Wilson, Betty Compson, Alice Terry, Alma Rubens, Anita Stewart and Viola Dana. Ingenues like May MacAvoy, Madge Bellamy, Mae Marsh, Mary Miles Minter and Jobyna Ralston competed with vamps like Theda Bara, Louise Glaum, Valeska Suratt, Carmel Myers, Barbara LaMarr, Olga Petrova and Nita Naldi for the attention of the heroes of the day. These included Richard Dix, Rod LaRocque, Charles Ray, Thomas Meighan, Conrad Nagel, John Barrymore, and, after Rudolph Valentino's success, such varied types as Ramon Novarro, Ricardo Cortez, Antonio Moreno, John Gilbert and Ronald Colman.

With this nexus of talents, silent screen acting began to create a style of its own, which was more indigenous to the camera and which could emphasize the significance of a detail with the "closeup"—a glance of the eye, an inflection of the eyebrow, a repressed smile. A new realism, expressing emotion through the smallest possible gesture and look, supplanted the previously exaggerated, more romantic style of the theater to produce an intimacy never possible before.

In general, most stage performers coming to the silent screen had a style too broad to be successful in adapting to the new medium. The best screen actors were those with little or no stage experience who had nothing to unlearn. Chaplin, Pickford, Gish, Keaton, Valentino and Swanson developed a simplicity and artlessness which belied the considerable work that went into their performances. And, above all, they had *youth.*

The camera was not kind to older, established performers like Bernhardt, Mrs. Leslie Carter or Duse, who commented astutely upon seeing herself on the screen (*Cenere*, circa 1916), "I made the same mistake nearly everybody else has made…something quite different is needed [and] I'm too old for it. Isn't it a pity."

Some from the stage who did have varying degrees of success included Nazimova, Jane Cowl, Richard Bennett, Alice Brady, Billie Burke, Taylor Holmes, Julian Eltinge, and John and Lionel Barrymore. From the Ziegfeld Follies came beauties like Marion Davies, Lilyan Tashman, Billie Dove and, in the late 20s, Paulette Goddard. Opera lent Mary Garden and Geraldine Farrar for brief flings at filmmaking. Imported from Europe were the finest acting and directorial talents. Pola Negri led the parade, followed by Emil Jannings, Lya de Putti, Conrad Veidt, Renee Adoree, Arlette Marchal, Vilma Banky, Lars Hansen, Karl Dane, Greta Nissen, Nils Asther, Camilla Horn, Jetta Goudal, Maria Corda, Paul Lucas, Tullio Carminati, Lili Damita, and, of course, Valentino and Garbo. From Mexico came Ramon Novarro, Gilbert Roland, Dolores Del Rio and Lupe Velez. The ever-growing foreign film colony included top directors like Ernst Lubitsch, Victor Seastrom, Maurice Stiller (who brought Garbo with him), Josef Von Sternberg (who introduced Dietrich), Jacque Feyder, Dmitri Buchowetski, Paul Leni, F. W. Murnau, E. A. Dupont, and the English colony of Ronald Colman, Ralph Forbes, Edmund Goulding, Herbert Brennon and Frank Lloyd. Talking pictures were later to swell this list to even greater numbers.

This brief essay can only begin to sketch a picture of the young Hollywood in which began the creation of Gloria Swanson. The whole story of the environment from which she came would fill books. Her pictorial history which follows helps give a more complete description of the woman who alone of all the silent screen pioneers remains a beautiful and lasting symbol of that glamorous era.

Above: Swanson's father was with the U.S. Army. A grave, pretty little girl, she spent most of her childhood on army posts. "I was an army brat. I hung around adults a lot but was shy with children my own age."

Bottom: She matured into the young vamp (circa 1917) posed in a style that was to be revived in the 50s with great impact by famed photographer Richard Avedon. This photograph of Swanson would seem to be the inspiration for his *Harpers Bazaar* series of portraits of women, which emphasized the extremely long neck and bare shoulders.

This photograph of Swanson, which was taken during her tenure with Mack Sennett, shows a smile rarely seen then. "How I hated my teeth. They were so big and square that I always kept my mouth covered with my hand when I smiled."

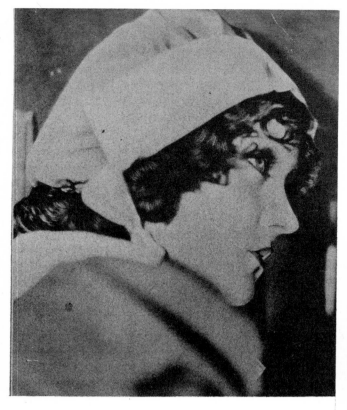

Swanson in the early twenties, during the period that she spent under the influence and tutelage of Cecil B. De Mille. Still shy and reserved, she usually presented a very serious, solemn façade to the world. At about that time, she said, "I have gone through a long apprenticeship...of being nobody....When I am a star, I will be every inch and every moment a star. Everyone from the studio gateman to the highest executive will know it." They did.

20

The young Swanson of the very early 1920s, the first glamour girl of the screen, who brought the word "glamour" into common usage. At first, her famous chin mole, which was to become such a trademark and so widely copied, was concealed by makeup. But by 1923, she accentuated it as shown in #4, a portrait in costume for *Bluebeard's Eighth Wife*, about which the then widely esteemed *Photoplay* commented, "nothing risque, nothing gained...one of Gloria Swanson's best pictures," and awarded her a "best performance of the month," an honor she was to receive fairly consistently for the next decade.

The gorgeously bizarre face, which has remained one of the great monuments of the twenties. Years later, Cecil B. DeMille said, "When you put them all together and add them up, Gloria Swanson comes out the movie star of all movie stars. She had something that none of the rest of them had."

In a 1964 interview, Swanson said, "I had the good fortune to be the one and only who made six pictures consecutively with him....He was an extraordinary man—great magnetism, great intellect, and with tremendous power and personality. He was a perfectionist who started the business of things being really authentic—a real ermine coat and real gems—all the lavishness in films.

"And he started another innovation—films about married people. Until then, they all ended with the engagement ring—or the wedding ring. We made *Don't Change Your Husband, For Better, For Worse* and *Why Change Your Wife?* all of which began a new vogue. I learned a great deal from him. He was a director who was *not* an actor who wanted to show you how to perform a scene as some directors do. He insisted that you act it your own way while he watched you very closely, saying, 'No, that was too fast, too hurried. Take more time. I didn't believe you when you did this or that.' It was great working for him because he didn't put his stamp on so many actors as Mr. Griffith did, so that the moment you saw them, no matter what picture, you'd say, 'Well, there is a D. W. Griffith actor'" (Radio interview with Werner Backer for N.B.R.).

 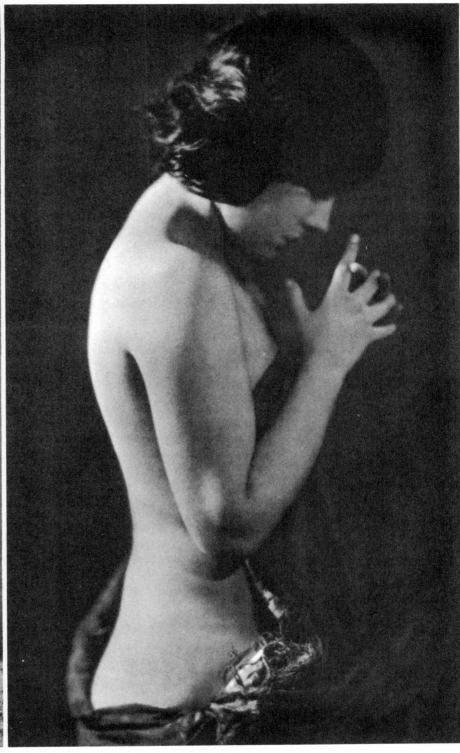

Gloria, draped and undraped by Alfred Cheney
Johnston, artist and famed photographer. At the
time that he took these photographs of Swanson
(circa 1920-1921), Johnston was chief glorifier of
the Ziegfield Girl and the highest paid glamour
photographer in the world. He was known as "Mr.
Drape" because of his flair for using all kinds of
draperies to provocatively adorn his usually scantily
clad camera subjects.

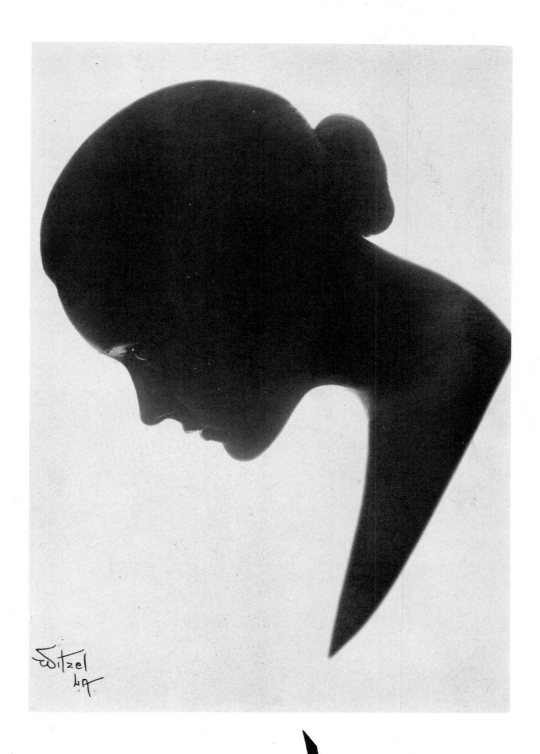

A very young Swanson,
who was about nineteen, is silhouetted above. Her unusual features,
so different from the pastel prettiness of her contemporaries, made her
a favorite of the camera, which found her extremely photogenic. She
managed somehow to combine the appeal of the ingenue (Lillian Gish,
Mary Pickford), and the allure of the vamp (Theda Bara, Mae Murray)
with the womanly qualities of a Norma Talmadge or an Alice Joyce.
Then, by adding a refinement and elegance of her own to the creation,
she emerged as someone new and different, and much more versatile
than any of the others.
◄ This gorgeous portrait was taken in 1922 about the time of
Her Gilded Cage. A resume of Swanson profiles covering a period
of forty years is presented on the last page of this section.

Early screen beauties tended to be categorized as *Ingenues* (nearly always blonde with long curls—Pickford, Gish, Minter) or *vamps* (exotic types, usually dark brunettes like Pola Negri, Nita Naldi, Theda Bara) or the *womanly* faces of brunettes like Norma Talmadge, Betty Compson and Alice Joyce. Chic departures from these three groups, like Swanson and Irene Castle, were more difficult to classify.

MARY PICKFORD

MAE MURRAY

INA CLAIRE

MARY MILES MINTER

MADGE BELLAMY

LILLIAN GISH

MAE BUSCH

MABEL NORMAND

NORMA TALMADGE

THEDA BARA

AILEEN PRINGLE

BARBARA LAMARR

Left page is Marion Davies, chatelaine of William Randolph Hearst, who began her career as a Follies Girl, then became a silent screen heroine and finally graduated to an excellent light-comedienne. On this page, top, are vamps Nita Naldi and Estelle Taylor, and, bottom, Jetta Goudal.

To "The Blue Book
of the Screen"
most sincerely
Gloria Swanson

The English authoress Elinor Glyn created a literary sensation before World War I with her then daring novel about
love and sex, *Three Weeks.* Brought to Hollywood in 1920 to
write an original screenplay for Swanson, Mrs. Glyn had a
considerable influence on the appearance and manners
of Gloria during this association. In 1922, she wrote another
story especially designed for Swanson and Rudolph
Valentino. Scenes from the second film, *Beyond the Rocks,*
are shown on the following pages. It had a flashback to an
earlier, more romantic period so that Swanson and Valentino
could appear in the picturesque clothes of the 19th century.
Glyn said of Swanson, "I feel she has an old soul struggling
to remember its former lives—not young like this great
America."

I've always been impressed by the exquisitely graceful use that Swanson makes of her small hands. She uses them as though ballet-trained. Remember her fantastic descent down the stairs at the end of *Sunset Boulevard,* with the Medea-like posturing, as she imagines in her madness that she is Salome?

Zaza, 1923, was an outstanding hit for Swanson, who played a gamine-like Parisian soubrette in a part that gave her the opportunity to wear her hair in a style obviously inspired by Aubrey Beardsley and these marvelously outlandish costumes, which were designed especially for her by famed couturier Norman Norell. *Zaza* was originally a David Belasco stage play starring Mrs. Leslie Carter, next a Metropolitan Opera opus for Geraldine Farrar, then an early (1915) silent film with Pauline Frederick and, after Swanson, finally a rather lavish talkie with Claudette Colbert (1939). Swanson won huzzas for *Zaza* from N.Y. critics, and even stronger enthusiasm for her performance in her next picture, *The Humming Bird*.

The Jazz Age was the subject of Gloria's 1923 film, *Prodigal Daughters,* in which she played a headstrong flapper who, fed up with a dictatorial father, leaves her Fifth Avenue mansion to lead her own life in Greenwich Village. Sounds familiarly like today's younger generation, doesn't it?

Adela Rogers St. Johns, chief chronicler of Hollywood's Golden Age, in an article, "Gloria—An Impression" (*Photoplay,* September 1923), wrote that Swanson's interest in clothes began on the old Triangle lot in 1918 with a designer named Peggy Hamilton, who "had an eye for line, a vision for color and a genius for knowing what women should wear. Peggy saw Gloria, then a restless, unstable, unsettled personality and, with that sure instinct of hers—that Parisian training, perceived something of the Gloria to come, the butterfly still hidden in the chrysalis. Then began the transformation that made Gloria Swanson, to my own taste, the most irresistibly beautiful creature on the screen. I admit it. Insofar as looks are concerned, I would rather watch Gloria than all the rest of them put together. I never have any idea what her pictures are about— I just like to gaze at her."

At this time, Swanson was emerging from the grooming of her mentor, Elinor Glyn. Adela continued: "This association seems to be bearing fruit in a new finesse of manner and dignity of bearing. . . . I can think of no one on the screen whom it will interest me more to see ten years from now. When you look back on the way she has come and see what she has made of herself in the past ten years, it's utterly intriguing to think what she should be at the end of another decade. And she will be only thirty-four then—the prime of a woman's beauty and charm." The astute Mrs. St. Johns was quite a prophet, but not even she could possibly have foreseen the incredible events that were to take place for Swanson, her dizzying peaks and deep valleys during the next decade.

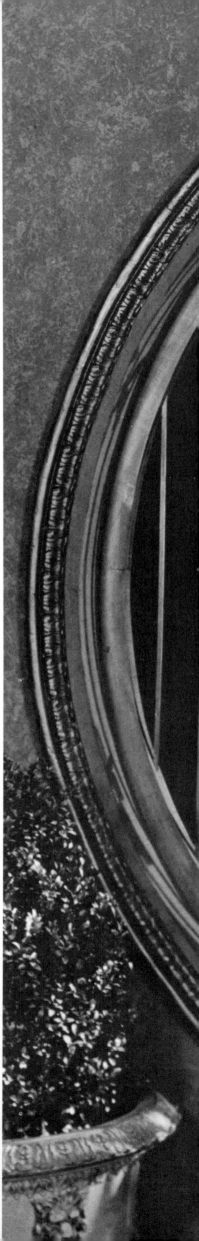

By 1924, a notable simplicity in Swanson's mode of dressing for the screen had taken place. Her cape and gown for *A Society Scandal,* for example, were a marked contrast to the elaborate costumes of previous years. Now that she was living and working in New York, her wardrobe and grooming reflected the taste acquired there. In 1929, the famous couturier, Captain Edward Molyneux, declared, "She is not only one of the best gowned women in the movies but in the world."

During 1923 and 1924, even critics who previously had considered Swanson pretty much of a clothes horse and an indifferent actress were forced to begin changing their attitudes. As a solo star with a string of consecutive hits, *Bluebeard's Eighth Wife, Zaza, The Humming Bird,* she was now also a critical success, having gathered plaudits that none of her contemporaries was achieving.

Then came her greatest success to date, *Manhandled,* in which she played a gum-chewing, subway-riding salesgirl toiling in a Macy's-Gimbels-like store. In the film, she did a brilliant impersonation of Charlie Chaplin and of a Russian countess, displaying a maturing subtlety in comedy and drama. Her hair was cut in a new, severe style, shown here—one which was to be revived in the mid-sixties by British hair stylist Vidal Sassoon. She was altogether an entirely new Swanson.

The startling transformation pictured here took place in 1924, evidence of Swanson's remarkable ability to change, her capacity for growth and refinement.
▲ Dispensing with all previous artifice, she becomes a fresh, new person, radiant, chic and even more beautiful with her famous *Manhandled* bob and altered mouth and eyebrows.
► Coiffured and gowned for *A Society Scandal.*

GLORIA AND POLA

By 1924, the battle for screen supremacy was being waged by Swanson and Pola Negri, the Polish star who had been imported from Germany by Paramount, which was also Gloria's studio. Negri had made a sensational success abroad, which she repeated in the U.S., with the Berlin-made *Passion* and *Gypsy Blood*, the former the story of DuBarry, the latter that of Carmen. Highly individual, she was also an excellent actress whose fiery performances and animal magnetism had the same impact on audiences that Anna Magnani' were to have three decades later. Whether or not the famous legendary Swanson-Negri feud had any personal basis, it *is* a fact that there *was* competition between the two for screen vehicles that culminated in Swanson winning a prize, *Madame Sans Gene*, which the studio allegedly had bought for Negri. Arriving in Hollywood in 1922, Negri had made seven films by the end of 1924, two of which, *The Spanish Dancer* and *Forbidden Paradise*, had matched her European performances and brought her a popularity the equal of Swanson's.

It was in 1924 that Gloria went to France to make *Madame Sans Gene* (the first time that a star went abroad to film a story in its native locale), married the Marquis de la Falaise and returned to Hollywood in triumph to snatch the crown of new Queen of the Screen as number-one box-office favorite.

Now there was also the much discussed question of social supremacy—Pola was a Polish Countess (having married Count Eugene Dombski while working in Germany), Gloria a French Marquise. Which ranked higher? The situation became more muddled when Pola married a Georgian Prince, the dashing Serge Mdivani, thereby upping her title of Countess to that of Princess! Was a Georgian Princess the social equal of a French Marquise? Hollywood argued and wondered. (A few years earlier, Rudolph Valentino and Pola had been best man and matron of honor of Mae Murray to David Mdivani, Serge's brother. Hollywood royalty marrying European royalty got the same worldwide attention in the 20s that the marriage of Rita Hayworth to Prince Aly Khan and of Grace Kelly to Prince Rainer were to get in the 50s).

The rivalry became too intense and so Gloria went to the more cosmopolitan atmosphere of New York to make her films, leaving Pola to dominate the studio in Hollywood.

Prior to this separation, however, there had been the famous alleged "battle of the cats" between the two. Primarily a press agent's concoction, one version was that Pola's path was crossed by a black cat so, obsessed by superstition, she had the animal caged and carried off the lot, whereupon Gloria, to keep her rival upset, not only returned the animal but had all the other stray cats she could find brought to the studio to run wild. Another version had Negri as the cat's champion, with Swanson being ailurophobic. It all got blown out of proportion to become a legend with both ladies vainly denying the stories. In a 1923 interview by Helen Klump in *Picture Play*, Gloria declared, "Next to being actually misquoted, I mind having little things exaggerated. The papers have made it appear that Pola Negri and I indulged in some common row over cats at the studio. We were pictured as squabbling little vulgarians. It would have seemed more fair if they had

printed the fact that Miss Negri had been a guest at my home—that I think her little foreign ways are fascinating—her accent delightful." Years later, in a 1964 TV interview (with Werner Backer for N.B.R.), when queried about Negri, Swanson answered, "She's just done another film [*The Moon Spinners* for Walt Disney] and I'm so happy about that." The interviewer asked, "I understand you had a feud for many years?" to which Swanson replied, "Honestly, what nonsense! No, of course not. The gossip columns started a lot of talk just to use up space, I suppose. Please bury this legend once and for all. I couldn't be happier that she's doing another picture. I think it's wonderful."

The fact remains that it will always be almost impossible to discuss the screen career of Gloria Swanson without referring to Pola Negri.

Four hit films in 1923 and five more in 1924 brought Swanson to a peak of incredible popularity. In November 1924 she sailed for Paris to film *Madame Sans Gene*, much of which was filmed at Fountainebleau Palace. There she met the young Henri, le Marquis de la Falaise de la Coudraye, who acted as interpreter and liaison for the film. They were married on February 5, 1925, in Paris, an event headlined around the world. The new Marquise soon became the acknowledged queen of the screen. When she returned to America with the Marquis, blasé

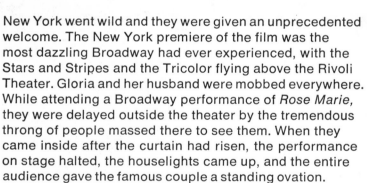

New York went wild and they were given an unprecedented welcome. The New York premiere of the film was the most dazzling Broadway had ever experienced, with the Stars and Stripes and the Tricolor flying above the Rivoli Theater. Gloria and her husband were mobbed everywhere. While attending a Broadway performance of *Rose Marie,* they were delayed outside the theater by the tremendous throng of people massed there to see them. When they came inside after the curtain had risen, the performance on stage halted, the houselights came up, and the entire audience gave the famous couple a standing ovation.

As they trained back to California, all across America signs waved "Welcome Home, Gloria" and similar greetings of proud affection for "Glorious Gloria," a home girl who had really made good on an international scale. In some towns, schoolchildren were given the day off so that they could go line the railroad tracks to watch "Gloria and Hank" pass by in their private train.

When the couple reached the coast, they made an entry into Los Angeles that was another production in itself. Some wag started the rumor that Gloria had wired ahead to Adolph Zukor, head of Paramount, "Arriving Monday with the Marquis. Arrange ovation." True or not, ovation there was!

Accompanied by the Mayor of Los Angeles, two brass bands and motorcycle escort, they swept triumphantly from the station to the studio, the streets massed with cheering fans. It was quite an occasion, even for a town used to the spectacular.

That evening, when she and the Marquis entered Grauman's theater for the premiere of *Madame Sans Gene*, the entire audience—comprised of Hollywood's great—rose to its feet applauding in a gesture of affectionate homage, and then sang, "Home Sweet Home." It was the greatest ovation that Hollywood ever accorded one of its own. Swanson commented, "It should have happened when I'm fifty. I'm only twenty-six. What's left? How can I top it?" (At fifty, she made *Sunset Boulevard*!)

The extraordinary scope of the metamorphosis of Swanson in just two years is illustrated here. *Top:* "Gloria and Hank"; *bottom:* a scene on the set of *Beyond the Rocks* (1923) with Elinor Glyn, Lady Henry and Mrs. John Hays Hammond. *Right:* Governor Howard M. Gore of West Virginia, director Allan Dwan, her husband, the Marquis, with Gloria in 1925. A movies clothes horse, elaborately costumed, had become a Marquise who dressed with the utter simplicity of great chic.

On the *left* and *bottom right,* Swanson at her home
at Croton-on-Hudson, New York, in 1925. *Above:*
Gloria, the Marquise de la Falaise, in 1926.
Her father was Joseph Theodore Swanson, of
Swedish-Italian descent. Her mother was Adelaide
Klonowski—Polish, French and German. This hetero-
geneous mixture of nationalities produced the
unique face that has intrigued for nearly sixty years.

An Amazing Marquise

The dignity of becoming the wife of a marquis is not going to have any effect on Gloria Swanson's screen rôles, apparently, for in "The Coast of Folly" she plays a part that promises to be one of her most dashing madcap accomplishments.

"The Coast of Folly" is a story of society intrigue in which the wealthy heroine is almost made the innocent tool of another woman's revenge on her husband. Fashionable and glamorous Palm Beach forms the background of the story.

PHOTO BY RICHEE

Gloria Swanson is a continual and refreshing surprise. In "The Coast of Folly" she appears for a short time in the little-girl outfit you see above with farcical results. But during most of the picture she plays the strikingly vivacious young girl you see in the other photographs on this page.

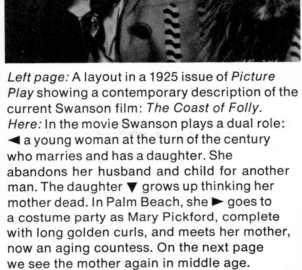

Left page: A layout in a 1925 issue of *Picture Play* showing a contemporary description of the current Swanson film: *The Coast of Folly.*
Here: In the movie Swanson plays a dual role: ◄ a young woman at the turn of the century who marries and has a daughter. She abandons her husband and child for another man. The daughter ▼ grows up thinking her mother dead. In Palm Beach, she ► goes to a costume party as Mary Pickford, complete with long golden curls, and meets her mother, now an aging countess. On the next page we see the mother again in middle age.

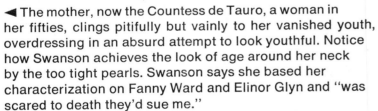

◄ The mother, now the Countess de Tauro, a woman in her fifties, clings pitifully but vainly to her vanished youth, overdressing in an absurd attempt to look youthful. Notice how Swanson achieves the look of age around her neck by the too tight pearls. Swanson says she based her characterization on Fanny Ward and Elinor Glyn and "was scared to death they'd sue me."

Three other Swanson portrayals. *Above right:* the temperamental opera star of *The Loves of Sunya* and (below) a beaten, prematurely aged school teacher. (This latter sequence was cut from the final version because of the film's length.) *Above:* Swanson's stage version of Barrie's *The Old Lady Shows Her Medals* gave her still another opportunity to pay old age. She did it so successfully that, at first, the audience did not even recognize her as the old woman.

Swanson was always a favorite model for artists of all types, photographers, painters and sculptors. Here are two drawings of her:
Left: a 1923 sketch by artist-photographer Hal Phyfe, who also did the stunning photograph 10 pages later.
Right: Artist-designer-director Hugo Ballin sketched Gloria in 1926 during the production of *Sunya*, for which he designed the settings.

Here is the Gloria Swanson of 1926–27, a woman who had reached the pinnacle of her profession and was the most copied movie star in the world. The vivid clothes horse of just a few years earlier had transformed herself into the luminous, beautifully groomed woman seen here. She had four establishments: a palatial Beverly Hills mansion, a sumptuous New York apartment, a country place at Croton-on-Hudson, and a château in Paris. She had a courtful of maids, secretaries, cooks and chauffeurs, elegant jewels, magnificent furs, gorgeous clothes. She had a titled third husband and a daughter and a son whom she would not allow to be photographed. She had just joined a distinguished group—Charlie Chaplin, Mary Pickford, Douglas Fairbanks and D. W. Griffith—at United Artists Studio to become her own boss, produce her own films, run her own organization.

Swanson moods from a 1927 portrait sitting
by Russell Ball, taken at the time of her first independent production, *The Loves of Sunya,* into which she
poured her Renaissance flair for lavishness and extravagance. Temperamental, dramatic and exciting, no
other actress topped her as everything that "movie
star" meant. When her contract with Paramount expired
in 1926, she turned down an offer to remain with that
company at $20,000 a week, 52 weeks a year, for five
years. It meant leaving the parent company, with its vast
training organization, its theater chain, its sales and
publicity department, to make her own films. Alone and
unaided, without the assistance that Mary Pickford,
Colleen Moore, Corinne Griffith and Mae Murray got
from their producer-husbands, she took the chances
and the consequences, never complaining afterwards.
There were always fresh goals. *Sunya* opened at the
new Roxy Theatre in New York but was not the hit
Swanson had hoped for. *That* success was to come with
her next picture.

A studio portrait of Swanson in 1928 at the time of *Sadie Thompson.* Her eye makeup with the heavily darkened lashes looks very contemporary (70s) while her hair style seems derived from a Velázquez painting. Swanson was refused permission to film Jeanne Eagels' great stage success, *Rain,* by the then guardian of film morals, ex-Postmaster General Will Hayes. Undaunted, she bought Somerset Maugham's original short story, *Miss Thompson,* and made *Sadie Thompson,* for which she received her first Academy Award nomination. ▶

Swanson's impact on the look of some of her contemporaries is illustrated here and on the next two pages. *Top right,* Joan Crawford, 1927, and Fay Wray, *left,* circa 1930.

Gloria Swanson 10

P184-687

75

Lupe Velez

Aileen Pringle

Pauline Stark

Pola Negri

Swanson

Olive Borden

Swanson

Fay Wray

To Laurence Carr
Avery good wish
Sylvia Brandon

Before the advent of Sound, Hollywood in the late 20s was presenting a wide variety of beauties, domestic and foreign. Among the top favorites were: EVELYN BRENT. *Below:* OLGA BACLONOVA BEBE DANIELS

Top—left, MARY ASTOR. *Right,* MYRNA LOY
Middle, VILMA BANKY, NORMA SHEARER,
GRETA GARBO
Bottom, LEATRICE JOY, GRETA NISSEN

The late 20s was also the heyday of Flaming Youth and Flappers. Leading exponents were (top) Clara Bow and Colleen Moore; bottom, Nancy Carroll and Ginger Rogers. Opposite page;
Top row: Joan Crawford, Alice White, Louise Brooks
Middle row: Madge Bellamy and Sue Carroll
Bottom: Germany's Lya De Putti and perennial Mae Murray

Two portraits from the legendary silent film, *Queen Kelly,* which was never completed. Swanson hired Erich Von Stroheim to direct his story of an Irish convent girl who falls in love with a prince engaged to the queen of a mythical country. When the queen discovers their ill-fated romance, she banishes the girl, who then goes to South Africa to live with her uncle. He dies, leaving her his estate, a brothel, where she, as the madam, becomes known as "Queen Kelly" because of her royal romance.

After being in production for a year at an investment of $800,000, Swanson decided to abandon the (silent) film when talkies arrived. Having been off the screen for nearly two years, she needed a hit picture immediately, for there were too many new favorites contending for her throne. Clara Bow, Norma Shearer and Greta Garbo were each being spoken of as the next queen, while Hollywood wondered whether she was washed up. Katherine Albert wrote: "An amazing woman ...who has had everything, lost it, then had it again, over and over....There is still a Swanson future, as there always has been. Something will happen, as it always happens to Gloria" *(Photoplay,* July 1929). As predicted, something did happen—*The Trespasser.*

Talking pictures debuted in 1927 and by 1929 nearly every big star had attempted a talkie with two exceptions, Garbo and Swanson. Swanson's silent contemporaries, Mary Pickford, Pola Negri, Corinne Griffith, Colleen Moore, Clara Bow and Lillian Gish were all victims of the change, and soon retired to be supplanted, overnight, by new favorites who could talk. A few silent stars emerged successfully from the fray: John Barrymore, Gary Cooper, Ronald Colman, Norma Shearer and Joan Crawford. Swanson went to work to see if she could join them.

She shot and finished a new picture, *The Trespasser,* in a fast, frantic six weeks. It was released in November 1929 and wowed everyone with the revelation that Swanson not only spoke her lines with ease and authority, but also displayed a remarkably professional singing voice. Once again, Swanson had surmounted overwhelming obstacles to triumph. *Vanity Fair* wrote, "A not too credulous audience at the New York premiere rose and cheered as the indomitable and really talented actress talked and sang her way back to screen prestige."

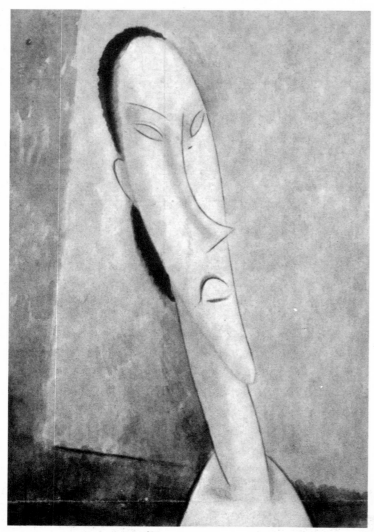

LADY WITH PARANOIA, AS BY MODIGLIANI

VEHICLE FOR A STAR, AS BY CHIRICO

Art in the image of Gloria Swanson

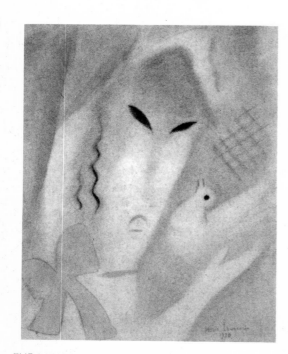

THE LADY OR THE DOVE, AS BY LAURENCIN

LADY WITH THE JITTERS, AS BY PICASSO

Covarrubias dons the mantles of five illustrious modern French painters

■ In each of these counterfeits of the work of five modern painters—the greatest, the most expensive and eccentric—Miguel Covarrubias has caught the lambent face of Gloria Swanson as it might issue from the studio of each. Here are the elastic attenuations of Modigliani; the cloudy Hellenism of Chirico; the odalisque in polka-dot shirt and plumes of Matisse; the dove, and eyeless smoke-lady of Laurencin; and the hangover geometry of Picasso. But, always shining through unmistakably, is the face of Gloria Swanson

Conde Nast graciously gave permission to reproduce these two pages from 1930 issues of that brilliant periodical, *Vanity Fair*.
Swanson is the inspiration for this amusing, clever travesty of the art field.
Right: An off-screen portrait by Von Horn, posed in her own clothes, a contrast to the glamorous screen raiment that women loved to see.

Robert Montgomery, artist Gaza Kende and his wife pose with Swanson in his studio during the painting of her portrait in 1930. The finished result can be seen 5 pages later.

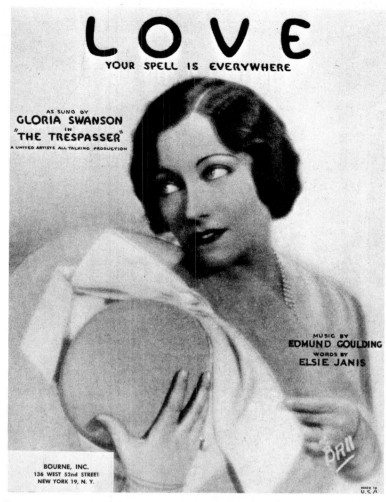

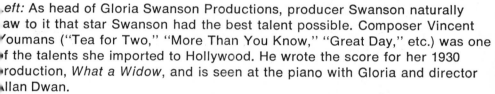

Left: As head of Gloria Swanson Productions, producer Swanson naturally saw to it that star Swanson had the best talent possible. Composer Vincent Youmans ("Tea for Two," "More Than You Know," "Great Day," etc.) was one of the talents she imported to Hollywood. He wrote the score for her 1930 production, *What a Widow*, and is seen at the piano with Gloria and director Allan Dwan.

Right: Gloria's glamour persists during her ever-changing appearance. *Below,* a 1930 portrait, and *right top*, a 1933 one. Notice her unusual bracelets, custom-made for her by Flato, which appear in other photographs of her throughout her section. *Right bottom,* Director Edmund Goulding, Gloria and husband Michael Farmer at the London opening of *Grand Hotel*.

1923 Hollywood

1933 London

Left: Swanson (circa 1933) with the finished portrait that was shown earlier. By this time, three years later, she had changed her hair style, her mouth and eyebrows to create another visage for herself, preparatory to a planned film with Clark Gable, a talkie version of Elinor Glyn's *Three Weeks.*

In 1931, Swanson married social-sportsman Michael Farmer during the filming of *Tonight or Never,* which introduced Melvyn Douglas to the screen. Upon completion of the picture, she retired from films for awhile, went abroad to line in Paris and in London, where she gave birth to daughter Michelle.

There she produced and also starred in *Perfect Understanding,* with Laurence Olivier as leading man and husband Farmer in a supporting role. She was absent from Hollywood for two years and returned in 1933 to find it a different place.

Leading Men: Left page, RUDOLPH VALENTINO.
Above, left, ANTONIO MORENO   ROD LAROCQUE.
Bottom, LAURENCE OLIVIER.

Other leading men included William Desmond, Elliot Dexter, Lew Cody, Thomas Meighan, Theodore Kosloff, Monte Blue, Wallace Reid, Harrison Ford, Ralph Graves, Huntley Gordon, H. B. Warner, Edmund Burns, Ricardo Cortez, Tom Moore, Ian Keith, Ben Lyon, Charles de Roche, Laurence Gray, Eugene O'Brien, John Boles, Lionel Barrymore, Walter Byron, Robert Ames, Owen Moore, Melvyn Douglas, Adolphe Menjou and William Holden.

The high wave of excitement attending her marriage to Michael Farmer had subsided after the intoxicating vacation of European living, the stimulation of Biarritz, the Riviera, Paris and London. The old hunger to go back to work, to act, to perform, to resume being *Gloria Swanson* and not just Mrs. Michael Farmer became too strong. Her two older children were put in school in Switzerland, free from the kidnap threats that Hollywood stars were experiencing then. So she prepared for a screen return.

When Swanson returned to Hollywood after her two years abroad, she had offers from the top studios, including United Artists, where she had produced her own films, and Paramount, her old studio of silent days. After considering all offers, she decided to sign with Irving Thalberg, head producer at M-G-M. After eight years of the trials, tribulations and heartbreaks of producing her own films, she found his offer, with the obvious advantages that a large, successful studio could give her, welcome and attractive.

It was considered daring but typical of Swanson that she would affiliate herself with a studio where she would be competing with Garbo, Crawford, Shearer, Harlow, Helen Hayes, Jeanette MacDonald and Marion Davies for top stories and directors. But she and Thalberg had great faith in each other. He announced that the first Swanson film at M-G-M would be *Three Weeks,* a talkie version of Elinor Glyn's book, which had previously been filmed silently in 1914 and 1925. He assigned Clark Gable, the top male star on the lot, as her co-star, and there was great enthusiasm and much publicity attending her "return."

She was sent to New York for some personal

appearances and radio broadcasts to publicize *Three Weeks* where she met actor Herbert Marshall (just as her fourth marriage collapsed). They soon began a romance and she filed suit for divorce from Michael Farmer. All of this coincided with the formation of The Legion of Decency, which was set up to combat the "alarming permissiveness in films" and the irreverent, cynical and immoral tone of them. Gangster films with their brutality, stories of prostitutes with frank scenes of bawdy life, and especially Mae West who flaunted her turpitude and didn't pretend to atone or reform—really shocked the women's clubs into angry action. The Legion was formed to combat immorality *on* and *off* the screen. An immediate change was felt: films were "Passed," "Objectionable in Part" or "Condemned." Players' private lives came under close scrutiny as women's clubs made their objections to the "flagrant and flamboyant" behavior of some stars.

The romance of Swanson and Marshall seemed to arouse a particularly violent complaint from the reformers. At the same time, producer Thalberg, always a frail man, became ill and was forced to take a recuperative holiday. The pros and cons of the situation were discussed, argued and written about, some saying that they had had enough of Hollywood's casual attitude toward marriage, others stoutly defending the right of performers to lead their own lives off screen. But the end result was that Swanson's film return was "postponed" until things cooled down a bit. It's amusing to think now of all that fuss and furore and the consequences, then to compare Swanson to Elizabeth Taylor, Vanessa Redgrave and Mia Farrow today and wonder what the Legion would have done about them. Times and mores *do* change, don't they?

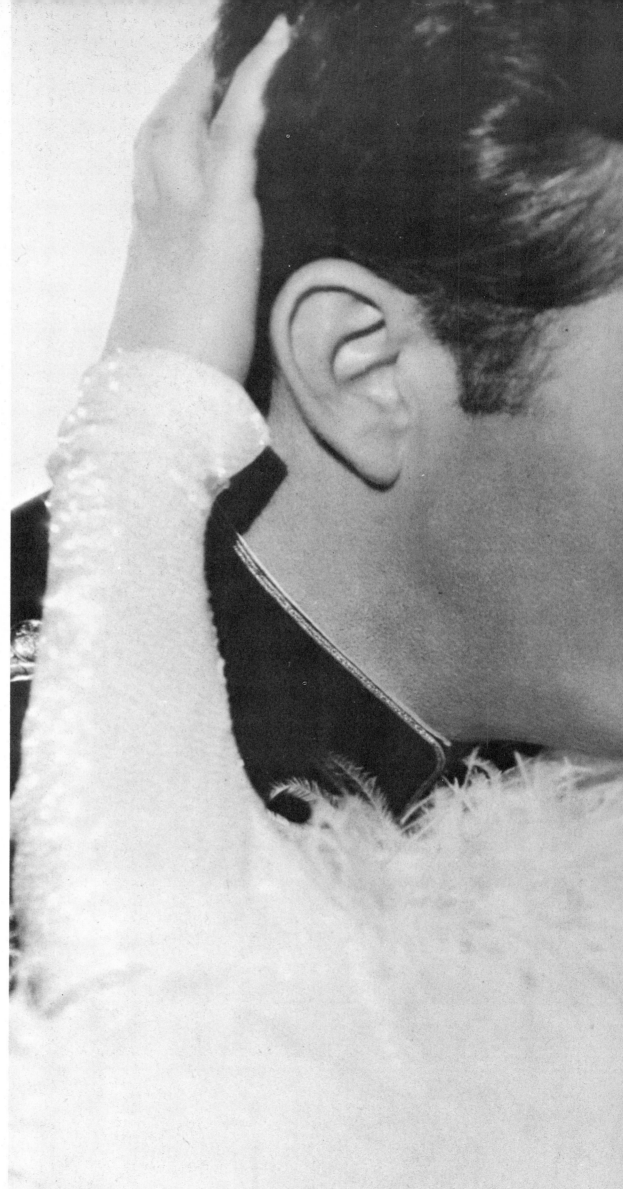

Swanson did return to the screen in 1934 in *Music in the Air,* the Jerome Kern–Oscar Hammerstein operetta with leading men John Boles, *right,* and Douglass Montgomery, *above.* As a glamorous, temperamental diva, she again displayed the genuinely lovely soprano voice that had been such a delightful surprise in *The Trespasser, What a Widow, Indiscreet* and *Perfect Understanding.* She also recorded for Victor and Brunswick records, sang on various radio shows, and later, in the 50s, planned a musical version for the stage of *Sunset Boulevard* that never materialized.

Left: After *Music in the Air,* 1934, Swanson was off the screen until 1941, though never out of the public eye. During this period, she was announced for several films by Columbia and by M-G-M, but the films were never made for various reasons.

Her seven-year hiatus saw her contemporaries busy making some of the outstanding films of that decade. Garbo appeared in *Painted Veil, Anna Karenina* and *Camille;* Crawford in *The Women, A Woman's Face* and *Susan and God;* Dietrich in *Desire, Garden of Allah,* and *Destry Rides Again.* The period also saw the rise and establishment of other stars like Hepburn, Mae West, Carole Lombard, Ginger Rogers—and great films for Myrna Loy, Irene Dunne, Jeanette MacDonald, Claudette Colbert, Kay Francis, Grace Moore and Norma Shearer. The screen had grown too large for there any longer to be just one Queen. By now each studio had a number of contenders even for the title "Queen of the Lot."

In 1926, *Photoplay* had written, "Ten years ago Gloria Swanson was an extra girl waiting outside the casting office. Today, she is a Marchioness whose salary is $20,000 a week." By 1936, Swanson was unemployed, with her screen future in serious jeopardy.

These portraits were of Swanson in *Father Takes a Wife,* her 1941 "return" film, charming but inconsequential. As usual, she had a new look—larger mouth (a la Crawford), different eyebrows (higher and thinner), and the hair styles of the early forties.

GS-151H

103

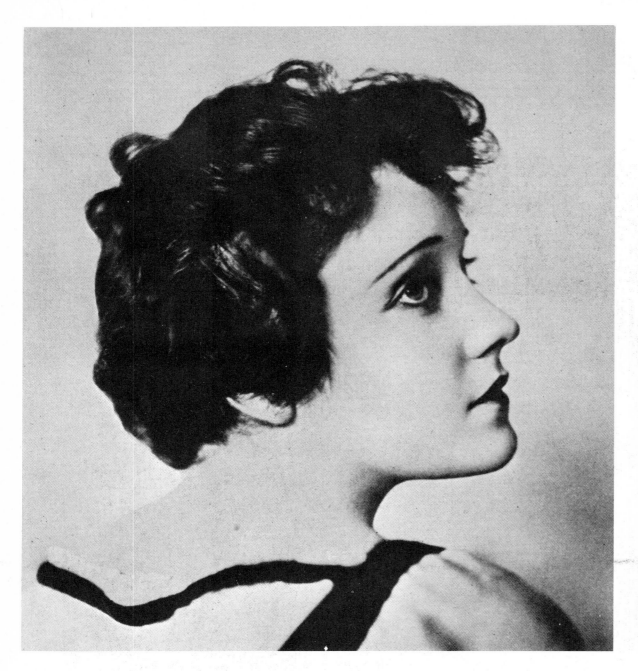

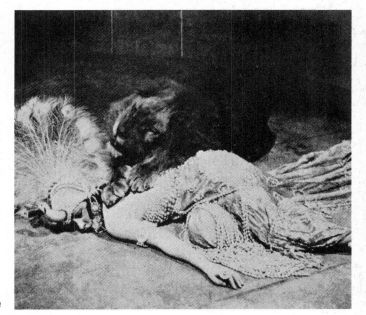 

Swanson's return to the screen attracted much attention from the press in national periodicals. Here are pictorial highlights of her career from 1915 to 1941, two pages reproduced from an article celebrating her "comeback" that appeared in *Vogue,* August 15, 1941. After this film, she was off the screen until 1949, eight long years during which she managed to keep herself and her name before the public. She appeared on radio's top shows like *The Rudy Vallee Hour, Hollywood Hotel,* etc., toured on stage in *A Goose for the Gander, Let Us Be Gay* and *The Old Lady Wins Her Medals.* She developed her other interests and business enterprises, a line of Gloria Swanson clothes, health foods, and Multiprises, a company which she organized to discover and exploit foreign patents.

Her beauty, flair for clothes, and ease of conversation led to "The Gloria Swanson Hour" on station WPIX, which opened with her as its big attraction on June 15, 1948. Her flexibility and familiarity with the camera made for a relaxed one-hour show five days a week. In early 1949, she returned to Hollywood to make *Sunset Boulevard.*

MARCUS BLECHMAN

In a 1932 interview, Mary Pickford said to Heywood Broun, "I don't think a star is really a star until he or she has lived through two slumps. When everybody says they're through—finished—and they come back twice, *then* they are stars."

How many times had Swanson come back? It's hard to count them all—but *Sadie Thompson* (1928) was a comeback after too long a decline. *The Trespasser* (1930) was another comeback after the ill-fated *Queen Kelly*. Following a long absence from the screen, *Music in the Air* (1934) was another comeback and *Father Takes a Wife* (1941) still another. But her fifth comeback in *Sunset Boulevard* in 1950 is unanimously acknowledged to be the greatest, most spectacular *comeback* in movie history.

For when Hollywood needed someone who could symbolize its most glamorous era, it chose Swanson for the part. And she was ready, giving a brilliant haunting performance with the dazzle and zoom of a fireworks display. Woven through this pyrotechnic brilliance was a deeply moving story. When the picture started shooting, it was about a struggling writer: when the picture was finished, it was the story

of a fading actress who went mad. William Holden and Erich Von
Stroheim were equally magnificent but the person who remained
indelibly etched in the memory was Swanson.

A new generation who had only read of a Hollywood long dead, a
place of white Dusenbergs, neo-Moorish bathrooms and titled con-
sorts, was bedazzled by the legendary beauty and glamour of the
woman who most personified that era. And everyone was overwhelmed by her performance, one of the most astounding feats of
histrionics ever seen on the screen.

To a man, the critics raved over her performance: "A tour de force!"
"She manages to pack every scene with more glamour than most
newcomers will pack in a lifetime." . . . "Gloria Swanson's portrait
of an aging screen star is one of the screen's great masterpieces.
Unquestionably! Here is a performance of such depth and
magnitude that it defies description." . . . "It's long since ceased to
be amazing that Gloria Swanson is amazing. It's only startling that
she can go on being more amazing."

Swanson's performance as Norma Desmond was so overpowering and dazzling that it awed and humbled Hollywood. Barbara Stanwyck, herself a superb actress, said to Swanson after seeing *Sunset Boulevard,* "I know where *my* place is—at your feet!" Groucho Marx exclaimed, "Here is the real place for that immortal line 'What Happened?' I feel like I've been hit by an earthquake." For her accomplishment, she received her third Academy Award nomination. But, as happens too often, the award went to a newcomer who duplicated a performance she had given on the Broadway stage. Jose Ferrer, Judy Holliday, Vivien Leigh, Karl Malden, Kim Hunter, Shirley Booth and Yul Brynner all have won the Award for performances they perfected while playing them previously on the stage.

It's a bitter irony that so many stars who helped create the motion picture industry and whose names are synonymous with it have never been rewarded for their distinctive achievements. Swanson, Garbo, Dietrich, Chaplin, Cary Grant, Irene Dunne, Charles Boyer, Henry Fonda, Orson Welles, Judy Garland, Edward G. Robinson and William Powell whose careers span many decades, are part of this long list. (Among the Award winners have been Harold Russell, Grace Kelly, Ernest Borgnine, Dorothy Malone, Red Buttons, Miyoshi Umeki, Burl Ives, Shirley Jones, George Chakiris, Rita Moreno, Julie Andrews and Lila Kedrova.) One feels like laughing heartily, like Gloria, *right,* on pondering this inexplicable enigma!

11454-

Like Dietrich, Swanson had quite a way with a cigarette. In her expressive hands, it became a descriptive part of the action. Remember *Sunset Boulevard*?

1923   1924   1924

1925   1926   1927

1928   1929   1930

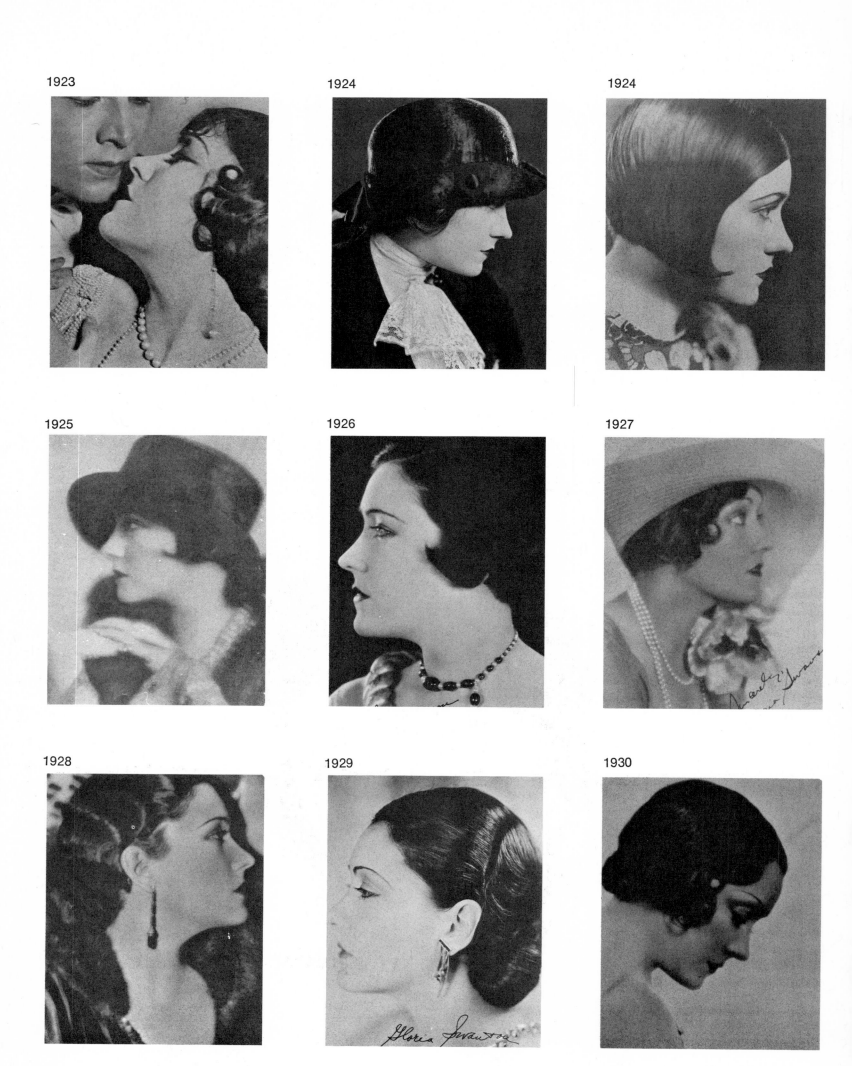

1931

1932

1933

1934

1941

1947

1950

1955

THE SIXTIES

This series of portraits, all taken by the sensitive New York photographer Marcus Blechman during the 50s and 60s, show the infinite variety of moods and expressions that Swanson has at her command.

Informal shots of Swanson with:
Publicist Wally Cedar
Director Chuck Walters
Fifth husband William M. Davey
Fourth husband Michael Farmer
Hedda Hopper, Marlene Dietrich, Lady Guernsey
and Kathleen Howard

Gloria is seen with:
Daughter Gloria, Jr., and grandson
On the set of *Father Takes a Wife*
With Alex Liers
Daughter Michelle and son Joseph
Escort Ray Daum

Greta Garbo is the great exception!
At the very inception of her Hollywood career, she began breaking the accepted rules of behavior for any up-and-coming actress, and during her career, continued to resist stubbornly to what she was expected to do to become a success. She never made personal appearances, never appeared on the stage in this country, and never appeared on radio or TV. (She also never made a "comeback.") She gave as few interviews as possible, almost never posed for photographs outside of her necessary studio assignments, and remained a nonconformist in her social life, too.

At first, this was due partially to the fact that, ill at ease and confused when trying to learn English, Garbo said the wrong things and created the wrong impression for the image that her studio wanted to create. A key to her desire for privacy may lie in the following story that was told many years ago by Howard Greer, a top dress designer in Hollywood. He had his own shop to which came the leading actresses, including Garbo. He said, "We were talking one day between fittings—and I spoke of people I'd known in Paris: Sarah Bernhardt, Gaby De Lys, Yvonne Printemps and Cécil Sorel.

V

"Wide-eyed, Garbo asked, 'I suppose nearly everyone who is famous comes into this shop?' When I answered yes, she continued, 'Don't they ever frighten you? People always frighten me!' And no one was ever more in earnest. "She told me something of her early life and experiences in Sweden. As an aspiring actress, she had her favorites whom she wanted to see but they moved in another world. Suddenly, in too short a time, she became a celebrity in America before she'd learned to speak English with any fluency. She was not prepared for the lionizing. It embarrassed her. An American might be prepared for it, but she wasn't. She was panicky before the unavoidable things that went with fame" *(Modern Screen,* January 1934).

This insight into the thinking attitude of the then young woman, shy, gauche, and inexperienced, whose studio was grooming her as a glamorous, exotic personality— a woman of the world—helps to explain, I think, her bewilderment, insecurity and gloom. She retired further into herself after unsuccessfully trying to adjust to her new position as a celebrity.

It must be remembered, too, that Garbo's ancestors were farmers—plain rugged country folk. She came from a low-income working family, her father a poor day laborer. It has been written that her parents were never married —that her mother was a common-law wife (Hollis Alpert, *New York Times,* September 5, 1965). I don't know whether this is true but, in any case, Garbo was always very reserved about her family, avoiding any questions, and telling as little as possible. If there were no marriage between her parents, that would certainly explain her reluctance to talk about her background much more than the other reasons usually advanced—her shyness, her lack of education and her commonplace environment. Even before coming to Hollywood, there had been the tremendous influence of her director, Maurice Stiller, who tutored her in social as well as screen technique, influenced her outlook and behavior, and so strongly communicated his own distrust of news reporters that the impressionable Garbo followed suit. He laid down a detailed program of behavior for her. In any business deals, Stiller habitually said no when bargaining, and the effectiveness of this gambit was not lost on his pupil, for it was particularly agreeable to her phlegmatic temperament.

During her brief European film career, she had been managed, directed and dominated by Stiller. But in Hollywood, he was not allowed to direct her, and after being fired by M-G-M, he went to Paramount where he directed *Hotel Imperial* and *The Woman on Trial* for Pola Negri (Garbo was a great admirer of Negri's and was, undoubtedly, influenced by her style of acting), and *The Street of Sin* for Emil Jannings. When he was dismissed by Paramount, he returned, broken and ill, to Sweden where he soon died. The ill-equipped Garbo, no longer able to depend on his guidance, was forced into the new, difficult role of making her own decisions. She found it a grim task until John Gilbert, whose leading lady she was in *Flesh and the Devil,* introduced her to his personal manager, the astute Harry Edington, who was persuaded to take on Garbo as a client. He rearranged her contract dispute with her studio, advised a "no interviews" policy and protected her in every way possible. With his counsel, she quickly grew in stature as an individual and as an actress. As a performer, her rise was steady and inevitable, and many critics considered her the finest contemporary actress on the screen. Something about her captured both the public's and her contemporaries' imagination.

During the 1968 festival of Garbo films at New York City's Museum of Modern Art, overwhelmed as I was, like the rest of the audience, by Garbo's beauty and forceful personality, I still began to realize, as I saw her in film after film (some twenty-five in all), that she grew increasingly tiresome as an actress, that her performances were much, too much the same. Whether playing a Swedish prostitute in *Anna Christie* or a Russian noblewoman in *Anna Karenina,* the gestures, the character pattern, the performances were all too similar. (Of course, this is true also of most performers—particularly great personalities.) I wondered if perhaps she was not overrated as a truly great actress by her critics and public because of her tremendous and unique personality? Remember also, that during her career, one saw an average of only one or two Garbo pictures in a year—sometimes less—and so, thus paced, one was not so aware of this sameness. In pointing out my reaction, I have no wish to diminish her art—there is only an endeavor to peer through the myths and legends that have grown up about her and her films. In seeing a similar festival of Dietrich films, however, I was impressed to find that this sameness is not true of Dietrich; that, in fact, she was quite different in many of her perform-ances. On one double bill, for example, the quiet, under-played woman in *Morocco* was nothing at all like the flamboyant, tongue-in-cheek girl of *The Devil Is a Woman,* who was always yelling, scratching, pouting. And on another bill, the cold, reserved countess of *Knight Without Armor* was a bore, to me, whereas the sultry nightclub per-former of *Seven Sinners* was an uninhibited delight. She seemed truly four different persons in these films, although consistently beautiful and glamorous in all of them. I'm convinced that she has uniformly been underrated as an actress because of her beauty.

Therefore I was extremely interested, while doing research for this book some time later, to come across a rare, forgotten interview with Leslie Howard, the distinguished British actor, in which he discussed these two performers and, to a degree, corroborated my feeling that perhaps Garbo had been overpraised as "the greatest actress, the Duse, of the screen," while Dietrich, in seemingly effortless performances, had been consistently underrated, at least until recently when a new viewing of her old films brought fresh appraisal.

In 1933, Leslie Howard made theatrical headlines by turning down an offer to play opposite Garbo, an opportunity which most players eagerly sought. Queried, he explained:

"She is a most intriguing personality. A peculiarly dominating personality on the screen and that is exactly why I declined that part. I shouldn't hesitate to play opposite the most glamorous of stage actresses since a play can be depended upon to materialize as rehearsed. But a picture is different: added to the terrific competition of her personality—which no man has equaled—the film would naturally be cut to her advantage. And where would I be?"

Asked to compare Garbo and Dietrich, he answered, "I had the pleasure of meeting Marlene Dietrich a week ago. She is very beautiful and I enjoy her pictures because she is such a delight to the eye. From a critical viewpoint, neither is a great actress. Dietrich has been the more fortunate in having been trained carefully by a director who understands her perfectly. He taught her to be alluring and she has attained her peak in becoming a pictorial triumph.

"Garbo has succeeded on account of her marvelous personality. She might reach true greatness if she corrected some bad mannerisms. It is her own fault that she has been handicapped by inadequate direction, for she has scared everybody so that they don't dare to supervise her —to advise her when she is mistaken" (*Screenland,* September 1933).

What about some of her co-workers—how did they view her? Of course, for those employed by M-G-M, it was not politic to be too anti-Garbo; the studio would not appreciate that sort of publicity. Yet several contract players were quite frank when asked to comment on her. "Phlegmatic" was Marie Dressler's opinion, after working with her in *Anna Christie.* "I have never known her to express an interest in anything, except once when I suggested the life story of Christina, the Swedish Queen, as a vehicle for her. She was really enthusiastic about that! But except for that one occasion, she always seems totally uninterested in her surroundings, even bored." (Garbo did play Christina three years later.) "Oh, not a great actress, but, rather, an effective actress," declared Charles Bickford, after working with Garbo in the same film as Dressler. . . .

Dorothy Sebastian, who appeared with Garbo in two films, *A Woman of Affairs* and *The Single Standard,* had this to say: "I decided that I would just be myself with her. So when our director, Clarence Brown, introduced us, I said hello casually, for I was actually not much impressed. I must have betrayed my feelings because Greta asked, 'How do you feel?'

"'Tired,' I answered.

"'I do, too,' replied Greta.

"'Good,' I grunted, almost rudely laconic.

"'I'm glad you're tired,' Greta went on. 'I like tired people.'
We seemed to get along famously from then on."
Clarence Brown, who directed her in a number of films,
said, "Socially, I don't see her at all. Only when she
invited me to her home to work on a script did I learn
that I had been living directly across the street from her for
almost a year! She is shy, almost abnormally so, awkward
in meeting people. If any stranger watches her on the set,
she becomes confused and finds it difficult to continue
a scene" (article by Paul Hawkins, *Screenland*, June 1931).
Years later, to Kevin Brownlow—in *The Parade's Gone By*
(Alfred A. Knopf, publisher)—Brown said, "For me, Garbo
starts where they all leave off… [she] had something
behind the eyes that you couldn't see until you photographed it in closeup. If she had to look at one person
with jealousy, and another with love, she didn't have to
change her expression. You could see it in her eyes…
nobody else has been able to do that on the screen."
In an interview by Charles Dornton (*Movie Mirror*, June
1934), John Barrymore said of Garbo: "Her greatest
quality is her simplicity. She has it just as the greatest
actress of the stage, Duse, had it. Although possessed, too,
of a powerful personality, giving her supreme command
of every situation, Garbo never depends on it and, strangely
enough, doesn't even consider it a particularly valuable
asset. When she told me this, I was amazed! She feels that
acting is merely her job and she keeps everlastingly at it
in the making of a picture.
"I've never played with anyone so wholly conscientious.
When we were together in *Grand Hotel,* I marveled at her.
In playing with her, an actor never has any trouble knowing
what to do for she always does the right thing. Her
intelligence is like lightning, showing her to be not only
a woman of will but of ideas and brains. She comes right
back at you everytime, like mental tennis."
In 1930, Douglas Fairbanks, Jr., did a series of pen portraits
and impressions of people with whom he had worked
for *Vanity Fair* magazine. He had appeared with Garbo

in the 1929 film, *A Woman of Affairs* (the silent screen version of Michael Arlen's *The Green Hat*). Of Garbo, he wrote, "She is the foremost personality on a horizon of vivid personalities. She is unique in a profession that demands of its champions that they possess more personality than actual skill. . . . It is primarily her shyness that makes one feel that she is solemn and indolent. On the other hand, she has the stubbornness of her race. When she doesn't wish to do a thing, she never makes a scene but sits back quietly and will not budge an inch until she wins her point. On the 'set' she is very quiet and unfriendly. It is a surprising experience, after seeing her at the studio, to meet her that evening at a party. She is then, instead of the matured, sophisticated woman of the world, a young girl of about 23 years who has a fresh clear face and is all enthusiasm. . . . One could pass her on the street a hundred times and never notice her unless she wished it. Outwardly, she is an ordinary person whose personality is so foreign to the American standard that it is tremendously alluring. Her ability as an actress cannot be denied but the personality overshadows it."

So Garbo was described as enthusiastic—and phlegmatic; helpful—and indifferent; rude—and cordial; friendly—and aloof; a genius—and just a hard worker. She was probably all of them.

For many years, Mercedes de Acosta was one of Garbo's closest friends, exerting a considerable influence on her, broadening Garbo's horizons with her deep knowledge of and interest in literature, art, music and life itself. She probably knew Garbo as well as anyone and better than most until they drifted apart. Before Miss de Acosta died in 1968, she wrote of Garbo a discerning character analysis which I paraphrase: She is Nordic, very reticent, and runs true to type in that she is afraid to show how emotional she really is. She tends to become serious and melancholy when alone but among people she can suddenly be gay and full of fun. Her real tragedy is that she is so much the lone wolf that, no matter how much she is involved with other people and tries to be a part of their world, in the end she is somehow compelled to let go and pursue her own course.

She is a Virgo—high-strung, critical, intolerant and analytical. Everything is held up to be examined in her own magnifying glass. She has the Scandinavian characteristic of caution to a marked degree, drawing back because of suspicion towards people and life itself, and creating an underlying sadness that lurks beneath the surface even in her gayest moments.

Her standards of friendship are so high that few people can meet them, which has made for a self-imposed isolation. Despite her overwhelming fame and the lionizing which people attempted to give her, she kept her dignity and continued to lead an austere and solitary life. She would never permit producers, directors or her co-stars to overstep their professional relation to her.

She will always be Nordic with all its introvert characteristics—wind, rain, and dark brooding skies.

Most performers, particularly stars whose careers have endured for an unusually long time (like those of the three other women in this book), become mercilessly driven as they persistently pursue that career. Somehow, they need the adulation, the attention, the publicity, so much that they can endure and even enjoy the problems of a public life. Garbo couldn't—so didn't. She left the screen in 1942 after *Two-Faced Woman,* and at first her retirement was just a temporary one. Both she and the studio assumed that when "the right story could be found," when the war itself was over and the vast foreign market which was lost during it was regained, she would resume her career. There was no plan or intention to make her retirement permanent.

But the longer she stayed away, the easier it became for her to say no to ideas that were submitted to her for another film. She was learning to enjoy her new-found freedom now that she was no longer under obligation to work. (And she had been working since she was fourteen.) She was able to travel at will for as long as she liked, and began to relax socially as never before and to learn more about literature, poetry, music and painting. She had no financial problems since her years of thrifty living and her astute business sense had assured her of all the money that she needed. So she lost interest in her career and began drifting for lack of direction.

Her friends and fans consider her life the past three decades to be a shameful waste of a great talent. They deplore her abdication from the screen, her secretiveness ("Garbo would make a secret out of whether she had an egg for breakfast," a friend complained), her self-absorption and lack of real interests. She leads a solitary existence, walking, usually alone, the streets of the world in pursuit of something she never finds. In spite of or maybe because of this, she remains a unique figure, a living legend, a Fabulous Face. She is Garbo.

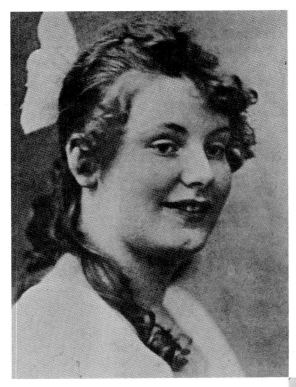

"The Story of my life? We all do the same things—we go to school. We learn, we grow up—one much as another. Some are born in mansions, some in cottages. What difference does this make in the long run? What does it matter who my parents were, or what they did? I cannot see what significance these facts have for others.
"I was always inclined to be melancholy. Even when I was a small girl, I preferred being alone. I hated crowds....Apart from skating and other winter sports, my best games were played by myself. I could give my imagination free rein—live in a world of lovely dreams."
This quote is from an interview with Swedish journalist, Oke Sunberg, given on Garbo's visit to Sweden in 1928 and later printed in his article, "That Gustafsson Girl" (*Photoplay*, April

1930). On that visit, she found her native countrymen to be as curious and insatiable for news about her as Americans and was besieged incessantly for interviews. The simple facts were that she was born on September 18, 1905, in Stockholm, the youngest of three children. At fourteen, she lost her father, whom she adored and resembled, and was forced to go to work as a banker's assistant. Later, she modeled hats for a department store, which led to a chance to appear in an industrial film. At seventeen, she auditioned and won admission to the Stockholm Dramatic School where she studied for two seasons, 1922–23 and 1923–24. At eighteen, she met Maurice Stiller who was forty, worldly and a famous film director. He was to change her life completely.

Two portraits from *The Saga of Gosta Berling*, Maurice Stiller's huge, rambling film (it originally ran over four hours) derived from Selma Lagerlof's discursive novel of the same name. Miss Lagerlof commented: "Mr. Stiller has seen too many poor serials"; but the film created a sensation in 1924 in Europe and introduced Garbo in the small role of Countess Elizabeth Dohna.

Only eighteen when the film was shot, Garbo was girlishly plump with only a hint of the extraordinary beauty that Hollywood was to appropriate and refine. Of Stiller, she said, "He compelled me to do what he wanted. I have him to thank for everything." Six years later, an obscure German actress was to make the same sort of comment about *her* director, Josef Von Sternberg.

Louis B. Mayer, of M-G-M, who w[as]
in Europe during the spring of 19[??]
saw *Gosta Berling* in Berlin where[?]
Garbo was filming her third and l[ast]
European movie, *The Street of So[r-]
row.* He offered Stiller a contract t[o]
come to Hollywood and Stiller
allegedly insisted on his protégé[e]
being signed, also. The tradition[al]
accounts of the deal have Mayer
different, even reluctant, to signi[ng]
the relatively unknown girl: he
wanted only the director. But the[re]
is also the theory that the astute
Mayer really wanted Garbo and, i[n]
order to get her, signed Stiller too[.]
In either case, Stiller handled all [of]
the details. Later, Garbo was to s[ay]
"Mr. Mayer hardly looked at me..[.]
he put a contract before me [and]
I asked Stiller if I should sign. I
always obeyed Stiller instinctively[.]
[he] told me to sign it so I did."
Garbo went home to Stockholm t[o]
prepare for the journey. She and
Stiller sailed for America from
Gothenburg in midsummer on the
steamship *Drottningholm*, and
arrived in New York on July 6, 192[?]
during an intense heat spell, whic[h]
they were to find unbearable. The
New York Times didn't even list
their names among the prominen[t]
passengers but did report that Po[la]
Negri had been fined $55,000 by t[he]
U.S. government for failure to de-
clare her jewelry on her last retur[n]
from Europe. Garbo read this rep[ort]
with awe: Negri was an idol of her[s]

Fewer than three years were involved in bringing about this amazing and almost unbelievable metamorphosis in the appearance of Garbo. The straggly eyebrows were plucked into a distinctive arch. The teeth were straightened and capped, the bushy hair brushed into the long, burnished bob transforming the unusual face, seen above in her first portrait sitting at M-G-M, in 1925, into the assured beauty on the right. Retained was her unique eye makeup, about which more will be written later.

The group of portraits in this layout were taken at one of Garbo's very first portrait sittings at M-G-M soon after her arrival in Hollywood. There was a charm and variety of expressions in the various poses which favorably impressed the studio heads, Mayer and Thalberg, who suggested dental work, new makeup, and especially a more attractive coiffure. After these steps were taken and her new grooming approved, Garbo was assigned her first role.

When these photographs were originally released for publicity purposes, the caption on one of them read, "Here is a study of Greta Garbo, M-G-M's new leading lady from Stockholm. At home, Miss Garbo is known as 'The Norma Shearer of Sweden'." The resemblance would seem to be mainly in the hair, or is it in the white fur?

After ten weeks of further tests and grooming, Garbo was finally cast in her first picture at M-G-M, *The Torrent*, directed not by Stiller but by an American, Monta Bell. Favorably impressed by the rushes of the film, Irving Thalberg, the 26-year-old "boy genius" of the film industry, began to take a personal interest in the career of "that new girl." Stiller secretly rehearsed Garbo at night, coaching her in every nuance he wanted her to express in the part, and keeping her securely under his wing. Studio officials began slowly to sense that they had inadvertently stumbled upon someone who might have a big future in pictures.

In the photograph above, one can see the original teeth that photographed so badly in closeup before her dental work was started. The marvelous seductive siren on the right gives evidence of the slimmer alluring beauty that was to come, the enigmatic magic that would intrigue movie audiences the world over.

Greta Garbo

Norma Talmadge

Reminiscent of several other stars at the beginning, Garbo for awhile was often likened to Norma Talmadge. Their similarity is quite apparent in these photographs taken in 1926. And how about the pictures on the right—can you believe that the coy maiden with the pursed lips is the aloof Garbo? The development of her face, figure and manner is an enthralling evolution as the "odd girl" becomes a world-famous beauty—a fabulous face.

Garbo's first American film, *The Torrent*, released early in 1926, evoked these comments about her appearance. Lawrence Reid in *Motion Picture* magazine: "A pretty, wistful and intensely feminine young person who suggests a composite picture of a dozen of our best known stars." Richard Watts, Jr., in the *New York Herald Tribune:* "She seems an excellent and attractive actress with a surprising propensity for looking like Carol Dempster, Norma Talmadge, Zasu Pitts and Gloria Swanson." *Pictures* magazine thought that "she possesses that which has heretofore only been laid at the door of Pola Negri—fire, animation, abandon.. . . She has a face that is strangely attractive, though not at all beautiful!" In these photographs, she looks like Pola Negri, Lillian Gish and Norma Talmadge. Within five years, most women were trying desperately to look like Greta Garbo, as shown later.

To the delight of Garbo and Stiller, he was
assigned as director for her second film, *The
Temptress,* and prepared for it enthusiastically.
But, as production began, there were immediate
problems: Stiller spoke no English and was too
impatient to use the interpreter at his disposal.
As expenses mounted during the endless delays,
the executives were perplexed by the film he
showed them and exasperated by his imperious
manner. After ten days of chaotic troubles, he
was dismissed and Fred Nible took over direction.
Garbo felt bewildered and pessimistic; with
Stiller in eclipse, she was all alone and out of
her depth.

When the picture was released, however, it was
another personal success for her. Robert E.
Sherwood, critic for *Life,* wrote: "Greta Garbo
in *The Temptress* knocked me for a loop . . .
[and] qualifies herewith as the official Dream
Princess of the Silent Drama department of *Life*."
Harriet Underhill in the *New York Herald Tribune*
thought that "Miss Garbo is not a conventional
beauty, yet she makes all other beauties seem a
little obvious." With each succeeding film, Garbo's
unique face was creating a new concept of
beauty, a special brand of allure.

For *The Temptress,* Garbo made her one and only personal appearance at the premiere, dressed in borrowed studio finery. She was introduced on stage by the Master of Ceremonies who said, "This is Miss Greta Garbo from Stockholm. Miss Garbo doesn't speak a word of English." "No," answered Garbo, unexpectedly helpful, "not von vord!" She was so embarrassed by the audience's laughter that she determined never to subject herself to the chance of its happening again. It was her first and last premiere appearance.

Below. A scene with Antonio Moreno.

While making her second film, *The Temptress*, Garbo met the great character actor, Lon Chaney, billed as "The Man of 1,000 Faces." Few people, except those who worked with him, knew Chaney personally: he would not appear in public and had no social life; fellow stars and studio executives were never invited to his home. He kept strictly to himself, would not work after five, jealously guarded himself, his privacy, his makeup secrets and techniques.

Garbo, a young woman of twenty-one just beginning her American career, was impressed by a star of the magnitude of Chaney. As they became friendly at the studio, Chaney perceived something of himself in the shy, withdrawn girl who also was a recluse. One day, he advised her, "Mystery has served me well—it could do as much for you."

Her natural instinct was to seclude herself anyway, so this counsel from an understanding and sympathetic friend made a deep impression on Garbo. It also made a deep impression on the M-G-M publicity department, which had been forced to cope with Chaney's uncooperativeness. It gave the department a direction to follow in handling Garbo who was already becoming a problem. Her conversation in limited English was hardly sparkling so that interviewers usually departed knowing little more about her than when they arrived. Ill at ease and suffering from an ingrained reserve, she became particularly speechless when their questions were of a personal nature, and such questions generally went unanswered.

To give Garbo a publicity "buildup" as "a woman of mystery" was a gratifying solution to what had seemed an insurmountable difficulty. Thus, the legend began.

GARBO—Metro Goldwyn Mayer

GGK-13

143

In the early forties before I went into the Army, I used to be a frequent guest of Mabel (Mrs. William) Le Baron's. She gathered small groups of friends, writers, painters, opera stars, musicians and film directors for her intimate dinner parties where the animated conversation ranged from the latest news to interesting reminiscences. One evening Max Ree, the Danish costume designer, told us a story about Garbo, whom he knew very well when he was doing the clothes for her early pictures, before Adrian took over that function.

Knowing Garbo to be lonely and to have only a few acquaintances, he had introduced her to a woman with a wide circle of friends and interests in hopes that she could help Garbo become better acquainted in her new environment. The two hit it off well on their first meeting, and as the woman got ready to leave, she proposed that they get together again soon, to which Garbo assented.

"Maybe we could have tea on Sunday?" the friend suggested.

"No, I don't like to have tea," Garbo responded.

"Oh," pursued the friend. "Then perhaps we could go for a drive, go visit some friends whom I'd like you to meet?"

"No, I wouldn't care for that," was again the reply.

Finally, after having several other suggestions turned down, the woman, who *had* agreed to try to help the lonely stranger, asked in desperation, "What *do* you like to do?"

"I like to sleep," answered Garbo. The woman, not being overly fond of afternoon naps, gave up her attempt to help and the new friendship died aborning.

Above: The *femme fatale* of *Flesh and the Devil.*

Right: The Temptress in which Garbo looked very Pola Negri-ish, an actress whom she greatly admired. "How I hate dose vamps, dose bad vomens! I want to play good girl," she protested.

Garbo began production of the silent version of *Anna Karenina* with Ricardo Cortez as Vronsky and Lionel Barrymore as Karenin. When the picture was half finished she became ill, forcing the studio to suspend shooting for several weeks until she recovered. Meanwhile, M-G-M had been deluged with demands from exhibitors and fans for another teaming of John Gilbert with Garbo after their terrific success in *Flesh and the Devil*.

So the studio scrapped the first version and reshot it with Gilbert replacing Cortez and Brandon Hurst as the husband. This modern-dress version carried the billing, "John Gilbert in *Love* with Greta Garbo." The lovely portrait, *right*,

is from the original production, while those on page 153 are from the second. After this, her fourth film, the studio decided to give Garbo star billing for the next film, "Greta Garbo in *The Divine Woman*," but in her third film with Gilbert, *A Woman of Affairs*, he still got top billing. During the filming of *Love*, Malcolm H. Oettinger wrote by all odds one of the most authoritative articles ever written about Garbo, entitled "Once Seen, Never Forgotten." Garbo had not yet banned all visitors from the set—remember, at that time she was only a leading lady. John Gilbert, open, gregarious, volatile, was the *star* of the film.

Oettinger said: "Without doubt Garbo is one of the most fascinating studies in allure ever introduced by stage or screen. She is the soul of passion, the embodiment of desire, a rare combination of ice and fire. However normal your respiration may be when you meet Garbo, you leave with a high temperature and a leaping pulse.

"She was in the arms of Jack Gilbert when I first saw her. The air was surcharged, the atmosphere glowed. As they embraced, unaware of anyone else, the heat curled the walls, blistered the chairs, all but stifled in its intensity.

"Slowly, Greta's arms encircled his shoulder, gradually she tilted her chin, suddenly their lips met. It looked for all the world like a closeup. In fairness to the interlocked pair let it be said at once that it *was* a closeup.

"But it was not received with the ordinary calm attending such routine affairs. Scene shifters edged nearer during the amorous passage! Calloused prop men paused to watch the tableau, script clerks blushed enthusiastically, and even extras awakened from their lethargy long enough to study the action....

"Gilbert, resplendent in the uniform he wore as Vronsky, in *Love*, was good enough to introduce me to Greta. Even with this auspicious start she was difficult to coax into conversation. For the first minute or two after Gilbert had withdrawn, I found my time taken up solely by her beauty. Perhaps it's not beauty in the strictest sense, certainly it is charm in its most devastating form. Greta's face is a pale oval with high cheekbones, smouldering eyes, sensitive nostrils. Her mouth is a crimson challenge. Her hair is blonde and smooth, carelessly arranged, but effective....

"She sits back and looks at you through heavy-lidded, half-closed eyes, her lips parted in a tempting smile, her slim hand daintily holding a cigarette. She is fully aware of her hypnotic influence, yet she says nothing to bear this out. She is sphinx-like in her silence, cryptic in her comments when she does talk.

"When she is acting, she seems totally unconscious of the audience behind the camera and fringing the set. She is unruffled, apparently natural, amazingly sincere in her interpretation. Technique, she told me later, she knows nothing of. 'I know the person I am in the picture, and I feel that I am that person for the time being. How I get what you call effects, I do not know....I do not know how I do it.'

" 'You are as beautiful as your pictures,' I said. This was no news to Greta. She smiled indulgently.

" 'I do not even say thank you,' she said.

" 'I'm not flattering you, I'm telling you,' I assured her.

" 'It is no difference,' replied Greta calmly....'I am not vamp. I do not know why they think I am....In Germany, I play sweet, innocent girls....Never am I wicked type. Here they say yes, I am. I do not like.'...

"Her voice is low and even, *basso profundo,* yet feminine at the same time. She is a girl in her early twenties who gives the impression of being a woman replete with worldly wisdom. No one could be quite as wise as Greta looks. She is Circe fresh from boarding school: Cleopatra, slimmer and less obvious than the popular version: she represents S. I., which stands for Sex Incarnate.

"Beneath her bland, unassuming exterior lies a shrewd intelligence. Greta may be an odd one: she may eat lunch in her dressing room, shunning the studio commissary! She may omit offers of roto-gravure portraits as mascot of the Los Angeles Rotary Club....But she has figured, I think, that unless she adopts an arbitrary, temperamental pose, bully-ng the officials to some extent, the officials will bully her.

" 'I do not like arguments,' she said, 'with shouting and fists banging....I go home. Then we do not argue....I will not play always the bad woman. They cannot force me, maybe I will rather do nothing at all.' A shrug and a slow, enigmatic smile emphasized this remark.

"Writing about the Garbo is unsatisfactory. She eludes description, defies analysis."

Garbo, in three short years, had advanced from the costumed leading lady of *The Temptress*, 1926, *left*, to the polished enchantress who was the star of *Wild Orchids,* 1929. By then, journalists were calling her "The Scandinavian Sphinx," "The Woman of Mystery" and "The Woman Who Walks Alone." Her fervent fans were described as "Garbo-Maniacs," a mild term for an adulation that bordered on the psychotic. Women, more than men, were guilty of excess hero worship: during the Garbo Festival in 1968 at N.Y.'s Museum of Modern Art, I saw some of this same sort of hysteria when the "Garbo-Maniacs" emerged again.

Katherine Albert, one of the head writers in publicity at M-G-M, wrote in *Photoplay,* April 1931: "I believe I'm safe in saying that Garbo has never expressed an opinion. I remember in the early days, when she was just beginning her career and I was in the publicity department, I used to go out on the set with what is called a symposium idea. This means that a writer for some magazine or newspaper has requested that I ask the stars for their opinion on various subjects. I grant you that some of these ideas were pretty terrible, but others there were that might have promoted a little interesting discussion.

"Invariably, Garbo said, 'Oh, dots silly. I do not vant to be quoted.' That was all right because she was, in those days, just beginning to build up that tremendous reputation for mystery. We weren't anxious to have Garbo quoted either, but I used to say, 'Very well, you won't be quoted but, just between ourselves, what do you really think about the question?' And Garbo *always* answered, 'Dots silly!' "

Irving Thalberg, M-G-M demi-god and Garbo's producer, had agreed with the theory advanced by her manager, Harry Edington, that Garbo should never talk to reporters, members of the press, or the public. 'I don't like to talk to people because I can't express myself satisfactorily. I don't say the things I mean,' Garbo had complained."

These 1929 portraits, made at the time of *The Single Standard,* helped whet her public's insatiable demand for more portraits of Garbo. Any picture, any scrap of information, was news.

Hollywood began to wonder what lay in store for Garbo as talking pictures became more popular. Her studio starred her in another silent, *The Kiss*, in late 1929, but her future was becoming a major problem.

MGMP-2051

Because of talking pictures, foreign importations like Emil Jannings, Pola Negri, Vilma Banky, and Greta Nissen were departing Hollywood in droves. A few tried the stage in an effort to learn to speak lines to the satisfaction of the demanding new medium but most returned to their homeland where their accents would present no difficulties.

Metro delayed Garbo's speaking debut as long as possible, finally selecting Eugene O'Neill's play, *Anna Christie*, in which a Swedish accent was a necessity. Breathless suspense was felt by her dedicated admirers as they waited to hear her voice. "Garbo talks!" billboards proclaimed. When the picture was unveiled, both her voice and her acting emerged triumphant.

Norbert Lusk, whose intelligent, much quoted reviews appeared in *Picture Play*, wrote: "The voice that shook the world!...Its individuality is so pronounced that it would belong to no one less strongly individual than Garbo herself." She had joined the small group of silent stars—Swanson, Shearer, Crawford, Colman and Cooper—whose voices assured them of continued success.

She is seen here with Charles Bickford, who played the Irish sailor who falls in love with Anna. *Above:* A rare still from the German version in which Salka Viertel played Mattie.

Romance, Garbo's second talkie, was a definite and decided contrast to the stark simplicity of *Anna Christie*. As prima donna Rita Cavallini, she was gorgeously gowned by Adrian in a succession of breathtaking costumes. Her "Empress Eugenie" hat was such an instant fashion craze that for a few months the women of America wore it constantly, until its incongruity with their Depression-length dresses finally penetrated their style sense.

The entrancing metamorphosis of the young Garbo of *Flesh and the Devil,* 1927, into the superb and splendid star of *Romance,* 1930, is seen in these two portraits. Her mouth was fuller, less girlish, her eyes more luminous, her manner more assured, commanding the attention and approbation of the senses. She had become a great and international sensation, admired by critics and idolized by a public for whom she had become the prototype of the "love goddess." She was unique in a profession of outstanding and accomplished performers.

Garbo's physical allure was seldom more eyecatching than in these four portraits. *Left:* the large, liquid eyes seem more mystically calm than ever, inscrutable and serene. *Above:* the magnetic Mona Lisa smile, assured yet inviting. *Right:* the lofty cheekbones, the fiery, volcanic eyes combine with a ripened mouth to produce still another mood. *Above top:* the incredible eyelashes, which were real, caused most other actresses to order tons of fake lashes hoping to achieve this same look.

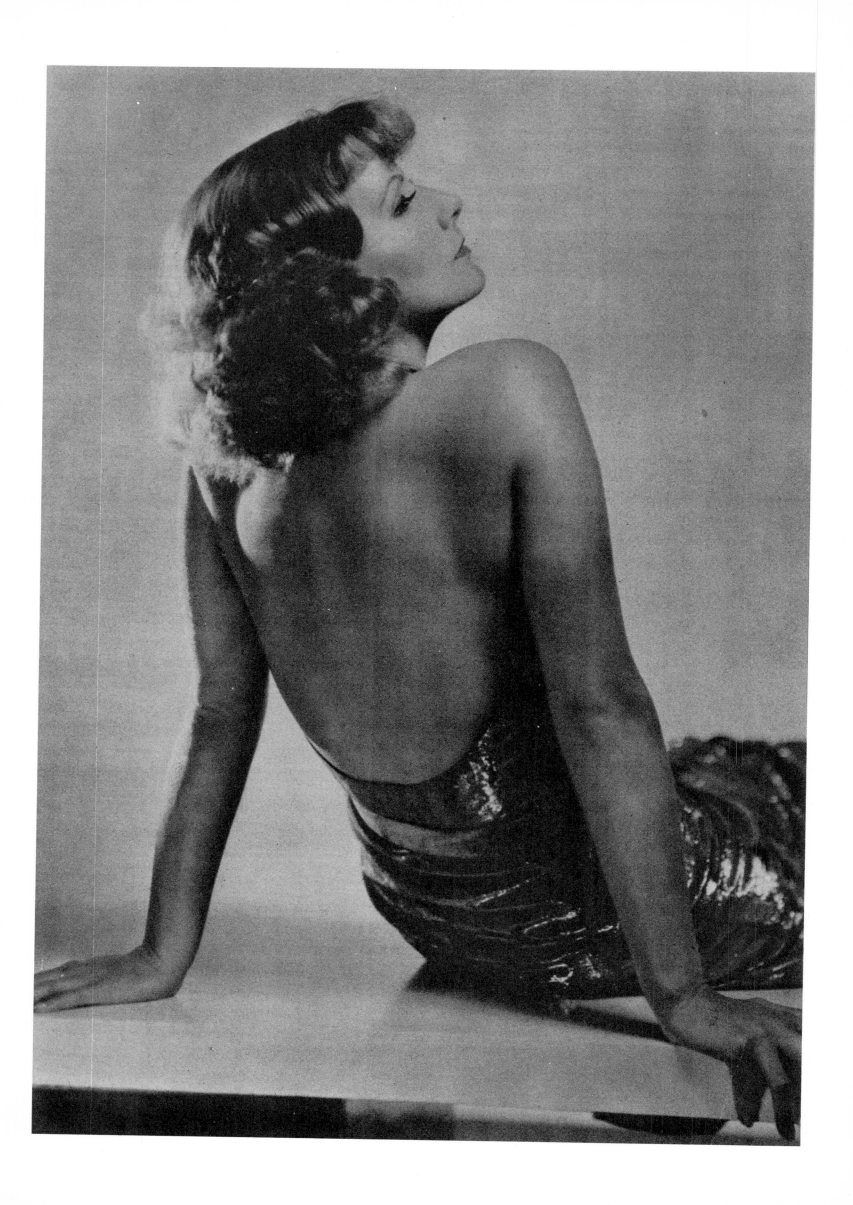

Clark Gable co-starred with Garbo in her seventeenth film, *Susan Lennox: Her Fall and Rise*, in which she wore bangs in some scenes. Half the women in the country, upon seeing the film, went home and immediately cut bangs for their foreheads.

Every decade sees a revival of the Garbo look. In the 40s, Ingrid Bergman and British actress Ann Todd tried it on. In the 50s, top model Ann St. Marie appeared in the pages of *Vogue* and *Harper's Bazaar* looking successfully and amazingly Garboish. Again, in the 60s, the slouch hat, beret, trench coat, etc., reappeared. It seems obvious that the look she created will continue indefinitely to influence the look of women.

GARBO - Metro Goldwyn Mayer   MC-195?

Mata Hari, Garbo's 1932 incarnation of the celebrated spy and dancer, was the source of these poses, taken by Clarence Sinclair Bull, her favorite photographer. After the untimely death of Ruth Harriet Louise, who took many of the earlier portraits of Garbo (and of Joan Crawford) in this book, Garbo posed professionally for almost no one else but Bull, who totaled over 2,000 portraits and stills of her in their sixteen-year relationship. A photographer of Hollywood's greatest stars for over forty years, he considers Garbo's face to be "the most inspirational I ever photographed."

Cecil Beaton and George Hoyningens-Huene, both consummate camera artists, agreed with C. S. Bull in placing Garbo at the top of their choice of beauties.

Beaton declared that, of all the women he had ever seen, "Miss Garbo is by far the most beautiful." Huene, in a discussion of screen beauties *(Photoplay*, August 1934), declared: "Garbo is unequaled and unparalleled...she is so far superior to any other woman on the screen that she has to be classed apart, not compared." (All three photographers included Swanson, Dietrich and Crawford in their choices of other supreme beauties.)

During her sixteen years and twenty-four films at M-G-M, Garbo played with most of Hollywood's top actors including:
Robert Taylor in *Camille.*
Lewis Stone in *Mata Hari* (Mr. Stone was in seven of her films).

Nils Asther, seen here in *Wild Orchids,* also appeared with Garbo in *A Single Standard,* both silent films. The teaming of Garbo and Clark Gable for *Susan Lennox: Her Fall and Rise* made for romantic pyrotechnics in their one appearance together.

BROWN·489
DANIELS
NITE SOUND

Among her other co-stars and leading men were Antonio Moreno, Lars Hansen, Conrad Nagel, John Gilbert, Robert Montgomery, Lew Ayres, John and Lionel Barrymore, Fredric March, Charles Boyer and Melvyn Douglas, and (seen here) *left,* Gavin Gordon, *this page,* Ricardo Cortez, Erich Von Stroheim and Ramon Novarro.

Garbo's fashion impact on women everywhere was tremendous: they copied her makeup style and look, and her shoulder-length bob. They wore her beret, her slouch hats and walked in the rain with trench coats turned up around their faces. Mannequins in dress shops, ladies of fashion, college and office girls, all found in Garbo a new pattern of beauty and style of dress, with the result that she altered the appearance of a whole generation.

With the advent of talking pictures, her accent made it necessary to cast her in European roles with foreign locales, dressed in a fashion difficult for the *average* woman to duplicate in everyday life. It was easier to imitate a Joan Crawford, a Katharine Hepburn or a Bette Davis than the exotic Garbo of *Mata Hari, Inspiration,* or *As You Desire Me.* Most of her succeeding pictures, *Queen Christina, Anna Karenina, Camille* and *Conquest*, were costume dramas, and the clothes did not lend themselves easily to adaptation for the working girl. But their influence was felt and fashion designers did adopt and simplify some of them.

Her "Empress Eugenie" hat from *Romance* appeared incongruous with the street clothes of 1930 but millions of women wore it nevertheless. The high collars designed for her long, slender neck and the accouterments she slithered about in as a Dutch spy, a Russian noblewoman or a Parisian actress might have been problems, but women wore them anyway, as Garbo remained a notable inspiration and influence.

LIL DAGOVER

KATHARINE HEPBURN

POLA NEGRI

ANN SOTHERN

BETTE DAVIS

INGRID BERGMAN

JOAN CRAWFORD

CLAIRE WINDSOR

Besides her fashion influence, the impact of the Garbo physiognomy during the 30s was sweeping and far-reaching. Established beauties Lil Dagover, Pola Negri, Claire Windsor and Joan Crawford, and newcomers Ann Sothern, Bette Davis and Katharine Hepburn all tried on the Garbo makeup and look. So did stage actress-dancer Katherine Sergeva, and ladies of society like Standard Oil heiress Millicent Rogers, famed for her extravagance, beauty, jewelry and wardrobe. (In 1949, she presented to the Brooklyn Museum a collection of her fabulous clothes.)

As evidenced here, all the ladies had eyebrows which grew high and were penciled above heavily lined eyes with enormous lashes; hair hung in a shoulder-length bob framing a face with high cheekbones and a mouth that was wide, sullen and weary. The Garbo look is revived every decade and I suppose and hope it will always be with us.

MILLICENT ROGERS

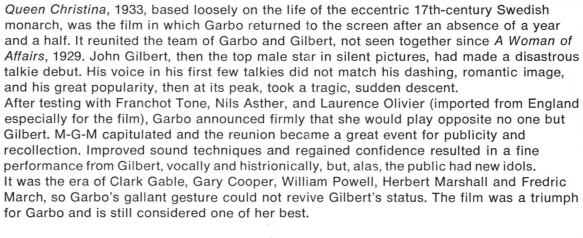

Queen Christina, 1933, based loosely on the life of the eccentric 17th-century Swedish monarch, was the film in which Garbo returned to the screen after an absence of a year and a half. It reunited the team of Garbo and Gilbert, not seen together since *A Woman of Affairs*, 1929. John Gilbert, then the top male star in silent pictures, had made a disastrous talkie debut. His voice in his first few talkies did not match his dashing, romantic image, and his great popularity, then at its peak, took a tragic, sudden descent.

After testing with Franchot Tone, Nils Asther, and Laurence Olivier (imported from England especially for the film), Garbo announced firmly that she would play opposite no one but Gilbert. M-G-M capitulated and the reunion became a great event for publicity and recollection. Improved sound techniques and regained confidence resulted in a fine performance from Gilbert, vocally and histrionically, but, alas, the public had new idols.

It was the era of Clark Gable, Gary Cooper, William Powell, Herbert Marshall and Fredric March, so Garbo's gallant gesture could not revive Gilbert's status. The film was a triumph for Garbo and is still considered one of her best.

The Painted Veil, a screen version of the story by W. Somerset Maugham, was notable for little else than Garbo's wardrobe, surely the most lavish costumes ever imagined for (her role of) the wife of a poor doctor (Herbert Marshall) stationed in China. Only a maharani could possibly have afforded the elaborate clothes in which Garbo suffered so bravely during a cholera epidemic. Needless to say, her fans loved it.

The portrait *above* was taken in 1930, the one *right* in 1934 at the time of *The Painted Veil*. Her hair has been described by Cecil Beaton as ''biscuit-colored and of the finest spun silk...clean and sweetly smelling as a baby's after its bath.'' Hers has been called ''The Face of the Century.'' No extravagance seems too high when one sees photographs like this: it is easy to understand superlative phrases like ''The Incomparable One,'' ''The Flaming Icicle,'' ''The Supreme Symbol of Inscrutable Tragedy'' and ''The mysterious, inscrutable, available but untouchable essence of the indefinable.''

The chiseled profile with the long, exquisite neck added to Garbo's lunar beauty. Throughout the years, photographers have delighted in vying for new ways to present its sensitive, touching nobility. These portraits range from 1927 to 1937.

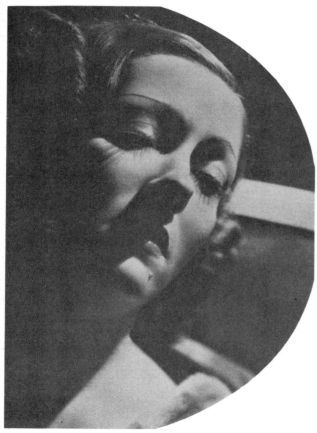

Garbo's extravagantly long eyelashes made an extraordinary design on her face, creating a dazzling composition of light and shadows which was not unnoticed by Swanson, Crawford and Dietrich.

Much of Garbo's appeal comes from her large, luminous eyes.
Deep-set and languorous, they are blue with full, dark irises,
and framed with lashes so long that they seem unreal. Her use
of her eyes for the camera was extraordinary; without changing
the expression of her face, she could convey the most subtle
thought with just a glance. They were an integral part of her
beauty and unique appeal.

Her makeup for the screen concentrated heavily on her eyes.
Unusual and elaborate, the makeup was an adaptation of a
design and style originally used on the stage to emphasize and
enlarge the eyes. First while the eyelid was closed, the eyeball
was outlined, then softened and blended. Next, a heavy black
line was drawn across the bottom of the lid to blend into the
eyelashes. At the corners, two additional lines were drawn
down and out, making a triangle, to extend their size and
shape (see illustrations).

815-X-14

In *Anna Karenina*, 1935, Garbo returned to the role of the tragic, lonely lady of St. Petersburg society in the 1870s that she had played eight years earlier in the silent version, *Love.* In her second impersonation of Tolstoy's heroine, Adrian gowned her in sumptuous furs, hats and costumes which enhanced her loveliness so that the critics to a man declared her more exquisite than ever. Her fine performance and beauty, plus an excellent cast and meticulous settings, could not altogether disguise the Russian "East Lynn" dullness of the picture and its excessive length. But who could quarrel with the mature magnificence of the radiant Garbo seen here?

Smiles!—M-G-M was rather succinct in its huge billboards that proclaimed to the world, ''Garbo talks!'' (*Anna Christie*) and ''Garbo laughs'' (*Ninotchka*). Here, it merely seems sufficient to say that ''Garbo Smiles.'' Others have written that when she smiles, ''she makes the Mona Lisa look like a D.A.R. receiving at tea.'' Norbert Lusk wrote, ''Her smile is a benison''; and Cecil Beaton, ''When she laughs she proves that things metallic have a soul.'' ''Her smile is a study in sophistication that renders the Mona Lisa's ingenuous by comparison'' (Malcolm H. Oettinger).

Camille, 1936, was Garbo's fourth costume picture and, most critics agreed, her best role and performance. "With fine intelligence and unerring instinct, she has made her characterization completely credible, while giving it an aching poignancy that, to me, is utterly irresistible," wrote Howard Barnes in the *New York Herald Tribune.* Robert Taylor was the handsome Armand, so passionately in love with the Lady of the Camellias.

For her performance in *Camille*, Garbo was nominated for her third Academy Award, an honor she was never to receive, but she *did* receive the New York Film Critics award for "the best feminine performance of the year."

Although the long, shoulder-length look is usually synonymous with Garbo, her hair was worn in hundreds of styles during her screen career, as one can see by checking through the Garbo section.

Garbo's twenty-fifth film, *Conquest*, 1938, was the story of Countess Marie Walewska of Poland and her romance with Napoleon, brilliantly portrayed by Charles Boyer. The public and most critics found Garbo "more beautiful than ever," as usual, a judgment which these portraits would seem to vindicate. But at least one reviewer, John Mosher, in *The New Yorker*, was not so mesmerized; he wrote that "Madame Garbo's elegant anemia, I fear, can pall a little."

Censorship resulted in a cause *célèbre* concerning *Conquest*, so four versions were prepared during a two-year argument about the screen treatment of Marie and Napoleon and their son; the censors, with a bland indifference to history, insisted that the final meeting of the three should represent "a forceful illustration of the tragedy of having been born out of wedlock." The result was a distortion of history costing $2,800,000, a gigantic amount for that time.

Garbo's majestic beauty would seem worth at least part of that sum.

The happy, smiling Garbo of *Ninotchka* (1939), *left,* is quite a contrast to the woman seen n this page in *Two-Faced Woman,* 1941, which was Garbo's last film. The studio tried o transform the lovely, world-weary woman so beloved by her fans into an American bomph girl," but the attempt and the film met with little success. Beset by censor roblems, poor reviews and an inauspicious reception, the film was a professional setback or Garbo, and she made up her mind to withdraw temporarily from films until after the war.

The large portrait, *left*, is from *Two-Faced Woman,* 1941, and the one *above* from *Inspiration,* 1931. Although her beauty had certainly not diminished in the decade between the two photographs, her hair and makeup had changed.

With her eyebrows heavier, her mouth larger, and her hair a darker shade, she looked in some ways more like the early Garbo of Sweden and M-G-M in the mid-20s. To my knowledge, this portrait is from her last sitting at M-G-M, and since then, only her close friends Cecil Beaton and George Hoyningens-Huene have had the privilege of having her pose for them.

Joan Crawford has always been an incredible geyser of vitality, one of the few that Hollywood could never lick. With the diligence of a ditch digger, she became, and remains, a winner—a champion. Her discipline, dogged determination to be the best, and her unlimited capacity for hard work are matched by very few— very, very few. Swanson has it, Dietrich too, although at different levels. Hedda Hopper, talking of Joan's drive, said, "I've known her since she made her first picture and there is a demon inside her. She cannot stop going, she cannot stop doing—she will never stop learning."

When you think back on her at the beginning—the Hotcha Kid, terribly young, laughing too loudly, showing off rather crudely, with her frizzy hair and bad clothes—and compare that girl with the methodical, systematic woman who plans every minute of her day, and who, like Dietrich and Swanson, awes co-workers and technicians with her knowledge and mastery of her craft, you get some picture of the terribly long, heartbreakingly hard road she has traveled.

Louella Parsons always said that "Joan Crawford manufactured herself," and that while other stars have, of course, changed themselves and their personalities, Joan *created* herself and her personality. Miss Parsons thought that Crawford drew up a blueprint, decided what she wanted to look like and sound like, and then put that person into existence.

Adela Rogers St. Johns once described her as "the highest voltage of personal impact—like taking hold of a live wire."

Joan has said, "Nobody's willing to fight today. Everybody wants a shortcut and I'm afraid there aren't any." She is a woman who has had four husbands, adopted four children—and who now lives alone, wearing her loneliness like a badge. "I've never had an ounce of self-pity, and I'm not about to start now"—with a flash of flint and steel. Veteran star Joseph Cotten, in speaking of Crawford, Davis, Swanson, Del Rio *et al.*, called them all amaranths—a non-fading flower. "Don't you think it's a lovely word for them? Abe Lincoln once said, 'Anyone over forty is responsible for his face.' These ladies wouldn't look the way they do if they weren't what they are."

VI

In the excellent book, *The Celluloid Muse*, by Charles Higham and Joel Greenberg, four of Crawford's directors speak highly of her ability and professionalism. Two of them, Robert Aldrich and Curtis Bernhardt, "compare Bette Davis vis-à-vis Joan Crawford, for many years her runner-up and rival as Hollywood's greatest post-Garbo star." Robert Aldrich, who directed her in *Autumn Leaves* and *Whatever Happened to Baby Jane,* said of *Baby Jane,* "I had always been a Joan Crawford fan.... Right from the beginning, Bette Davis and Joan Crawford were my two choices for the movie roles.... The two stars didn't fight at all on *Baby Jane.* I think it's proper to say that they really detested each other, but they behaved absolutely perfectly ... never an abrasive word ... not once did they try to upstage each other."

Curtis Bernhardt *(Possessed)*: "Compared with Bette Davis, Joan Crawford was as easy to work with as can be.... The chief difference between Crawford and Davis is that, while Davis is an *actress* through and through, Joan is more a very talented *motion picture star* ... just as professional, she is also simpler."

Jean Negulesco, director of *Humoresque,* once said, "It's difficult to get what you want out of her because she has such definite ideas, but in the end, the result is so satisfying that she could be one hundred and ten times more difficult and I'd still be happy.

"She is a very effective actress, and so much a star that her acting spills over into her private life.... Everything for her is acting: this is her life, her food, her drink. She gives herself completely to any part she has to play."

George Cukor, known as Hollywood's top woman's director (Garbo, Hepburn, Bankhead, Judy Holiday, Bergman, Garland, Ava Gardner and Audrey Hepburn), directed Crawford in three of her best films, *The Women, Susan and God* and *A Woman's Face.* He said, "Joan Crawford was very easy to work with, very sensitive.... In the first half of [*A Woman's Face*] when she played a facially scarred criminal, I thought she displayed great gifts ... she's a very accomplished actress and she realized that the part was 'twisted.' Right before every scene, in fact, she'd try to 'twist' herself mentally.... The situation was so strong that it had a great deal of style when she played it that way."

Though she has the power of complete concentration, still her awareness of the camera—her sensitivity to any photographer—is so acute that when he aims his lens (although she may be deep in conversation) she instinctively turns her best face and the nearest Pepsi bottle so that the label will face the camera. Some have said that after playing Joan Crawford for over forty years it's doubtful whether there is any private personality left. She works very hard—and very competently—at making people like her, and her precise handling of the press is a testimony to her many years in the business. While in Boston to plug a picture, for example, she raced through nine newspaper interviews, seven radio tapes, two TV tapes, and one newsreel, at the same time autographing pictures and posing for innumerable photographs in an unbelievable three hours and nine minutes. "It should have been done in an hour and a half," she said after everyone had left.

She's still a real, old-time movie queen—tough, positive, regal, imperious, with those throaty commanding tones. Crawford's tart, Texas tongue, the pitiless icy voice, at which producers, directors and co-stars have all trembled one time or another, are part of Crawford—part of the stormy life she has led—another side of the calm, gracious, poised woman which she shows in public. She still has the figure with the broad shoulders and slim lines which set a clothing fashion for two decades and a style among American women for forty years. She has great admiration for what she calls professionalism—but only severe scorn for those without the discipline to stick to a job and do it well. Years of hard work and professional preoccupation with the way she looks have helped her to preserve the illusion of youth. Co-actors comment on her "professionalism," her unflagging concentration (and call her a real trouper). She's a perfectionist who knows exactly what she wants—and she usually gets it.

This is Joan Crawford at about age eight, in Lawton, Oklahoma. She was born in San Antonio, Texas, in 1904 and baptized Lucille Fay LeSueur. Her parents were divorced while she was an infant and her mother then married Harry Cassin: by the time she was nine she was called Billie Cassin (*opposite*).
A close look at those huge, round eyes should silence forever the rumor that she had them slit to enlarge them for the screen. Makeup did *that* trick.
She kept that appealing half-smile to the left for nearly four decades until a steely discipline perfected an absolutely straight smile. I find the original so much more captivating: you'll see it throughout the early part of the Crawford chapter.

In 1925, when the screen was still very silent, a twenty-one-year-old dancer arrived in Hollywood for a try at the movies. She was pretty but so were hundreds of other girls who stormed Hollywood yearly by the carload. She was not an actress, nor was she particularly ambitious to be one: she just wanted to dance and to have a good time. Her childhood had been lonely, her background humble. She had waited on tables to put herself through school, but dropped out during her first year at Stephens College at Columbia, Missouri, so that her education was scant and her tastes undeveloped. Her show-business background was equally meager: she had been a chorus girl for a few short years at the Oriole Terrace in Detroit, at the Friars Club in Chicago and at the Winter Garden in New York City in the back line of *Pretty Ladies*. There was little to distinguish her from dozens of other girls under contract to the studios. M-G-M then knew so little about her that the original caption on the back of one of these photographs reads, "This is Lucille LeSueur, who is known for her lovely brown hair."

People told her that she looked a little like Gloria Swanson (*left*) and like Pauline Frederick, two top stars in 1925. The other notable female stars then were Corinne Griffith, Norma Talmadge, Mary Pickford, Colleen Moore and, at her own studio, Mae Murray and Lillian Gish. As her screen education began, she would learn something from all of them.

Introducing Lucille Le Sueur Who Needs Another Name for Her Screen Career

Name Her and Win $1,000

But Before Reading the Contest Rules on Page Six, Read This Interview with Her

By Joan Cross

"I'M QUITE thrilled over this contest which is to find me a new name," smiled pretty Lucille Le Sueur across the luncheon table, out at the Metro-Goldwyn-Mayer Studios.

"People never have been able to pronounce my name or spell it," she continued, "and I told Mr. Harry Rapf, when I found that, through this contest the readers of Movie Weekly were to choose a new name for me, that I personally will favor one which is easy to pronounce and spell, and also easy to remember. Of course it must be a pretty name as well."

I pass on this hint of Miss Le Sueur's preferences, as it may prove valuable in guiding contestants in the Movie Weekly Contest. Miss Le Sueur is but one of the judges, and, of course, the majority will rule, but her preferences will be seriously considered, for, after all, she's the one who will wear the name.

If you're planning to enter the contest—as indeed who is not—I'm sure you'll be interested in knowing something about Miss Le Sueur, herself. She is an auburn-haired, blue-eyed beauty and is of French and Irish descent. Second only to her career is her interest in athletics and she devotes much of her spare time to swimming and tennis.

Miss Le Sueur was selected by Mr. Harry Rapf, official of the Metro-Goldwyn-Mayer company, as being the ideal young American girl of today. Mr. Rapf interviewed hundreds of girls in New York recently, in the hope of finding new faces and developing new talent for the Metro-Goldwyn-Mayer stock company. Mr. Rapf firmly believes in giving new people an opportunity on the screen, but first they must impress him as having outstanding personalities and latent talent. Of the many girls who took tests in the hope of being sent out to Hollywood, Miss Le Sueur was the only one to be awarded a contract with the Metro-Goldwyn-Mayer company. You can readily understand that she is an exceptionally attractive young lady, to have won this honor. So great is Mr. Rapf's faith in her that she will be given an important role in "The Circle," the noted stage play soon to be filmed.

Miss Le Sueur was born in San Antonio, Texas. She was always ambitious to go on the stage, and used to put on her

Her parents would not consider a theatrical career for their only daughter, and as all her pleadings were in vain, Miss Le Sueur took matters into her own hands last spring and ran away from school, landing in Chicago with just two dollars.

She applied for a place in the Ernie Young Revue, where her youth and beauty won her the opportunity to do a specialty number. The revue went presently to Detroit, where it was presented at the Oriole Terrace.

While in Detroit, "Innocent Eyes," starring Mistinguette, also played in that city, and Lee Shubert dropped in one evening to see Young's Revue. The famous showman immediately singled out Miss Le Sueur as being a young lady of talent and charm, and what was her [delight] next day to receive an offer to join the "Innocent Eyes" company.

With this show, she went to New York City, appearing at the Wi[nter] Garden there.

Miss Le Sueur says that she had never thought of a motion pict[ure] career up to this time. Her ambition was rather toward the music[al] comedy stage, and she seem[ed] rapidly headed toward stard[om] there.

But one day she heard a group of girls discussing the chances of getting into motion pictures. Someone said that Mr. Harry Rapf, of Metro-Goldwyn-Mayer, was in town, taking tests of scores of girls and young men, with the intention of augmenting his stock company on the Coast. For the first time it occurred to Miss Le Sueur that she might like to become a film actress, and she arranged for an interview with Mr. Rapf.

"When Miss Le Sueur came into my office," Mr. Rapf tells me, "I knew that she had that rare thing—personality. She is beautiful, but more essential than beauty is that qual[ity] known as screen magneti[sm]. Even before we made came[ra] tests of her, I felt that she pos[-]sessed this great asset. He[r] tests proved it."

(Continued on page 31)

mother's dresses and act roles before her mirror when she was just a child. When she grew older, the family moved to Kansas City, Missouri, where she attended St. Agnes' Academy, and later she was sent to Stephens' College, at Columbus, Missouri.

"When I heard that I had passed the screen tests," Miss Le Sueur said, "it seemed like a dream. My mother is now reconciled to my career, which she objected to at first, and is in Hollywood with me. And when the readers of Movie Weekly decide upon a screen name for me, my happiness will be complete."

Talking of her, Mr. Rapf says: "When she came into my office, I knew that she had that rare thing —personality. She is beautiful, but more essential than beauty is that quality known as screen magnetism. Even before we made camera tests of her, I felt that she possessed this great asset. Her tests proved it."

All Photographs by Bull

If you're planning to enter the contest—as indeed who is not—you'll be interested in knowing something about *Miss Le Sueur* herself. She is an auburn-haired, blue-eyed beauty and is of *French* and *Irish* descent. Second only to her career is her interest in athletics, and she devotes much of her spare time to swimming and tennis.

Mr. Rapf selected her as being the ideal young *American* girl of today.

And her first starring role will be in "*The Circle*," a screen version of the noted stage play.

The almost unbelievable transformation in this face from the girl on the left to that on the right took place in less than a year and shows clearly the early and continuing search that Crawford was to pursue for many years for an identity of her own. The hair and eyebrows were the first to change. The magazine pictures on the preceding page illustrate the now-legendary contest that transformed Lucille LeSueur into Joan Crawford. The original winning name was Joan Arden, but when a real Joan Arden showed up at M-G-M, the second name was selected, one which Crawford disliked so much that for the next three years she called herself "Jo-Anne."

Adela Rogers St. Johns, Hollywood's top chronicler, wrote: "The first time I saw Lucille LeSueur was a memorable one to me.... I was knocked off my feet by her resemblance to Pauline Frederick, to me the most all-around attractive woman of her generation. So when I walked out on the M-G-M lot one bright morning and saw crossing the sweep of lawn a young girl who, in some uncanny fashion, turned back the clock to the days when Pauline Frederick conquered New York, I got tremendously excited. Here was the same beauty...winged feet and hidden fire...[and] air of pride that had thrilled theatre and movie audiences of Miss Frederick.

"The disappointment in meeting Miss LeSueur was correspondingly great and, I realize now, correspondingly unfair. Obviously, it wasn't fair to expect an untrained, inexperienced kid only a short time out of the chorus to have the full-fledged beauty and mentality, culture and poise, wit and wisdom that time, contacts and hard work had given Pauline Frederick." These photographs of the girl whom Adela met show that "beauty and fire," but give little indication of the face to become famous a few years later.

During her first few years as a stock contract player, among the assets Joan Crawford had going for her was the fact that she was extremely likable, frank, fun and good-natured. Most of all, she was cooperative. Just ask Joan and before you could say Metro-Goldwyn-Mayer, she would pose for anything you could dream up. The result was that she quickly became a favorite of the publicity department and began appearing with increasing rapidity in every magazine in the country. (This was at the same period when Garbo wouldn't pose for *any* publicity.)

But Joan would and did! She posed winning

Charleston dancing cups, racing whippets, autos and trains; reading papers, poetry and pamphlets; fondling dolls, dogs and diaries. She posed as a pirate, a Spanish senorita, as Hamlet, and a sailor's sweetheart; she christened battleships, joined the marines, met visiting dignitaries. Movie exhibitors and fans began to ask for more of that girl with all the pep, and her career began to ascend.
◀ Joan being posed by Ruth Harriet Louise, M-G-M's top photographer, who took most of the early Crawford and Garbo pictures in this book. With James Murray on location for *Rose Marie*. Her unquenchable vitality is apparent in every picture. (bottom right)

The Joan Crawford of 1926 was described in two articles thus: "She shimmered in a blazing spotlight...incandescent —intense—brittle—feverishly pursuing fun."

"When you see Joan do the Charleston or the St. Louie hop, or the tango, or whatever crazy dance happens to be in at the moment, you think of her as the symbol of everything the younger generation is supposed to be....You look at her and automatically stock phrases come to mind: Bobbed hair—rolled stockings—defiance—topless roadsters... 'Hey, Hey'—Jazz—short skirts—slang—little hats banged over one eye—high heels and all the rest."

Here are six pictures of that symbol of flaming youth at the time of those descriptions, a girl looking like six different people. By 1927, she had been leading lady for every male star on the lot, playing opposite Charles Ray, Lon Chaney, John Gilbert, Ramon Novarro, William Haines and even Jackie Coogan. Her appearance changed from film to film as, not yet important for the studio's top grooming, she experimented to her heart's content with whatever makeup and hair style caught her attention. After stressing her resemblance to Pauline Frederick, she switched to imitating Gloria Swanson. Her brown hair was dyed black, red, blonde—every conceivable color variation and style: long, short, up, then down.

Her eye and mouth makeup was just as varied, and a "new Joan Crawford" appeared in the papers and magazines every month. The innate ability to dramatize herself in every situation was a big asset until she began to carry it to extremes. She meant it every time she changed and believed fully in every role she assumed until the next one took its place. These rapid transitions were not always easy on her co-workers and friends who sometimes found it difficult to keep up with her rapid metamorphoses.

When these photographs were taken in 1928, Joan was leading lady for William Haines in *West Point*. Ann Sylvester described her in *Picture Play*: "She chose the beautiful name of Joan and pronounces it Jo-Anne....She has a little habit of making engagements and forgetting them....She gets a frightful bill from some impatient creditor and on the same day entertains ten girls at a high-priced restaurant....Her mind is quicker than a trigger, but uncultivated....She can't make up her mind whether she wants to be like her current idol, Corinne Griffith—or continue her present wise-cracking way. One moment she is broadly sounding her vowels, the next she's racking herself with a laugh that can be heard beyond the city limits. She's a funny kid alright."

Within five years, Crawford was to become famous for her punctuality, her prompt payment of bills, her mental inquisitiveness and that well-modulated voice with its overtones of Kansas City, Mayfair, and Beverly Hills.

Joan's extraordinary resemblance at times to Gloria Swanson is quite apparent in the portrait on the left: she has copied the Swanson smile, the look in the eyes, and even the Swanson chin mole.

MGMP-3538

At the time of *Our Dancing Daughters*,
interviewer Malcolm H. Oettinger had this to
say in an article entitled "Portrait of a Wow!"
"No man looks at Joan Crawford without
looking twice. That is a nine-word portrait of
a wow. One might catalog the red hair and
the challenging smile, the confident eyes and
the impudent chin: one might go into statis-
tical ecstasies over the figure, matching it
against that of the Milo…and still it wouldn't
be enough…she is youth personified, verve
itself, snap and zip and springtime. She is
what the public wants."

Our Dancing Daughters was the turning point in Crawford's career. It was a box-office smash and made her studio realize that she was ready for stardom. In it, Joan was a windblown flapper, dressed by Adrian. The sets, designed by Cedric Gibbons, created an architectural sensation: they were the last word in *art nouveau* and *moderne*. With this film, Crawford challenged Clara Bow, the *It* girl, for first honors as the personification of modern young womanhood, and became the idol of millions of girls who copied her every gesture, costume and makeup change.

1928

When Crawford's many assets are being discussed and enumerated, somehow her exquisite nose is seldom mentioned. The eyes, eyebrows, mouth and hair seem to overwhelm one's attention. So take a look at the nose, beautiful from any angle, straight, classic, and an important part of a remarkably photogenic face.

Dancing was always a part of Joan Crawford's life as she grew up. "I loved to dance...the only time I felt I belonged was when I was on the dance floor." When Joan was a small child, her step-father, Henry Cassin, managed a vaudeville theater. "I was stagestruck from the first. It was entrancing to watch the dancers backstage....Once a ballerina in flaming-red tarlatan let me kneel before the lighted mirror on her dressing table while she put purple eye shadow and pink rouge on my face. I inhaled the smell of greasepaint, the musty scent of scenery, the dancers flying about....I literally danced through the days....I never walked." After her mother divorced Cassin, she saved the chance coins that rare winds blew her way to see any show in which dancing was the motif because it symbolized beauty, motion, grace and drama. In her apprentice days in Hollywood, she would watch Mae Murray at work at the studio, admiring her "for the tremendous discipline over her body... every facet of her dancing technique came to bear on her performance....I began to realize that I wanted to become an actress, maybe a dancing actress."

By 1930, when these pictures were taken, Joan and dancing were synonymous in the mind of her public which had watched her win Charleston and Black Bottom contests and achieve stardom with *Our Dancing Daughters*.

merica's Dancing Daughter fell in love with Holly-
ood's young Crown Prince, Douglas Fairbanks, Jr., in
28. The screen's Royal Family, Mary Pickford and
uglas, Sr., were not very pleased about the romance
d refused to receive Joan at Pickfair, their home.
e couple were engaged for a year until their marriage
New York on June 3, 1929, attended by his mother,
s. Jack Whiting and a few close friends. The once
lie Cassin, who worked her way through school
iting on tables, the once Lucille LeSueur, Charleston-
ntest cup winner, had now become Mrs. Douglas
rbanks, Jr., a member of filmdom's top family.
e had also just finished her first starring role in
r Modern Maidens, which had Doug, Jr., in its cast.
e wired M-G-M: "If I have worked hard in the past,
tch me now." They returned to Hollywood for Joan to
ke her first talking pictures, with a singing part in The
llywood Revue, and as the star of Untamed. Joan's
king debut was a decided success: some other
ppers, Clara Bow, Alice White, Madge Bellamy and
e Carol soon "retired."

Joan is seen here in an early talkie, *Paid*, 1930, and in an off-screen candid snap with Helen Wills, the tennis player. The new Mrs. Douglas Fairbanks, Jr., wore almost no makeup and dressed with utmost simplicity. The actual shape of the Crawford mouth can be seen in these two pictures, contrasted with those of the young glamour girl on the opposite page. She went domestic with just as much passion as she had poured into being a "Jazz baby," becoming quieter, more gentle, more reserved—with a steady deepening of character, poise and authority. The former Black Bottom hoyden now stayed home sewing her own clothes and hooking rugs: "Our Modern Maiden" graduated to "Model Wife." She listed as her favorite actresses Garbo, Gloria Swanson and Ann Harding.

good
one

The Crawford eyes and mouth were so
spectacular that her beautiful nose, fine high
forehead and exquisite profile (which I've
mentioned before) were often overlooked.
Here are two portraits that display these
features effectively: the one above by George
Hurrell, the one on the right by Clarence
Sinclair Bull.

253

(Circa 1930–31.) The plump, undistinguished girl who arrived in Hollywood in 1925 was being called "the perfect camera beauty" by 1930. In five years, she had radically altered her appearance: now exposed were the modeled bone structure, the fine forehead, the slender neck. Her dramatic eyes and mouth continued to capture attention. Crawford's rapid metamorphosis had by 1931 established her as one of the three top feminine stars at M-G-M. Only Garbo and Norma Shearer outranked her: Garbo had a large European audience, and Shearer was the wife of Irving Thalberg, the studio's top executive. The situation created a lot of jockeying for position and for top pictures. Crawford's constantly improved appearance and beauty, her excellent speaking voice and radiant assurance made her a match for the other two in spite of films that couldn't compare with her rivals'. While Garbo was assigned stage successes of the caliber of Eugene O'Neill's *Anna Christie* and *Romance*, and Shearer got prizes like *The Trial of Mary Dugan* and *The Last of Mrs. Cheyney* (which Joan was to remake in 1937), Crawford surmounted such unmemorable trivia as *Montana Moon* and *Our Blushing Brides*. It was certainly to her credit that the public flocked to see her in such lesser material, nevertheless.

In her continuous search for a beauty all her own, Crawford tried every hair color and style. In 1931, she went blonde, then blonder for *Laughing Sinners* and *This Modern Age*. Tanned, vital and sparkling, she made an instant impact; her popularity increased with every film. The woman with her, bottom left, is Pauline Frederick, her early idol, who played her mother in *This Modern Age*.

In her autobiography, *A Portrait of Joan*, Crawford says that early in her career Paul Bern took her to see Pauline Frederick on stage. "I watched her artistry, her confidence, her beauty. I wished I could make people love me as she made an audience love her." A few years later, Miss Frederick appeared in a Crawford film and Joan wrote, "Acting with Pauline Frederick was a stirring experience with me....I had the opportunity of knowing her, savoring her quality. Her voice...was just one adjunct of her charm, as were her physical beauty and dramatic ability." Above is a 1930 portrait of Pauline Frederick.

At this time, she defined her idea of beauty: "Pastel prettiness has never appealed to me, only vital beauty. The born beauty's perfection has a tiresome sameness while the attractive woman must work at it, making the most of each good point. Gloria Swanson, for example: her nose isn't classical and she has other defects according to artistic standards. Her superb assurance carries her as she has acquired the arts of grace and poise. Maybe a bit theatrical in her swank but a thing of flame. "Ann Harding's is a more tranquil beauty—it is spirituelle. Backing its delicacy is a note of vitality. She is so confident that she gives the impression of active drama even when she is still."

She included the newly arrived Dietrich, who had just been seen in *Morocco* and *The Blue Angel*: "Marlene Dietrich has a childlike spontaneity—she acknowledges every introduction by springing to her feet and shaking hands vigorously. Her naturalness charms me and her naiveté, which is pointed by her own vivid color."

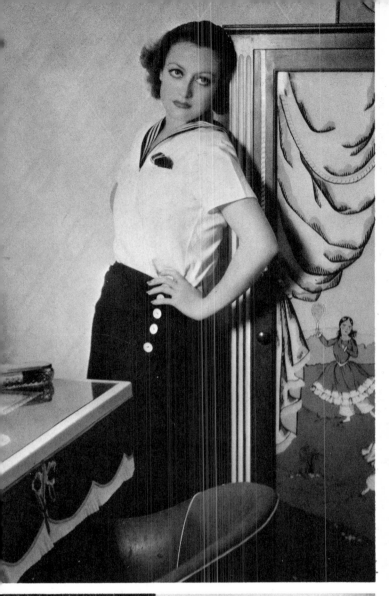

By 1932, Crawford was running neck and neck in popularity with the great Garbo. Her long string of hit pictures, plus three excellent and critical successes in a row, *Possessed*, *Letty Lenton* and *Grand Hotel* (which also had Garbo, John and Lionel Barrymore, and Wallace Beery as co-stars), had made her the most discussed and argued-about star on the M-G-M lot.

Then came a slight setback. Crawford fought for, and won, the much sought role of Sadie Thompson in *Rain* and was borrowed by United Artists for the picture. Five years earlier, Gloria Swanson had been nominated for an Academy Award for her silent version of Sadie in 1928. By 1932, the 1922 play seemed dated, and this second version drew mixed reaction. *Variety* thought "Crawford's get-up as the light lady...extremely bizarre," while Delight Evans in *Screenland* opined, "I think Joan comes close to greatness. She can no longer be considered only a spectacular movie personality...a brilliant, if erratic, performance and in several scenes, she rises to real heights."

After Joan Crawford played Sadie Thompson with her lips alarmingly enlarged by a new makeup style, the mouths of women were never the same. Gone forever was the small rosebud mouth beloved by their mothers; passé was the cupid's bow of the twenties, as women everywhere began to enlarge their lips, painting above and below the natural lipline.

Sadie has been a favorite role of other actresses: Jeanne Eagels had played her originally on Broadway in 1922; Tallulah Bankhead revived the play in 1935; June Havoc essayed a musical stage version in 1944; while Rita Hayworth brought the lady back in 1955 for an updated, third screen try. *Above:* Gloria Swanson as Sadie.

ADRIENNE AMES

MARION DAVIES

CRAWFORD

GERTRUDE MICHAEL

LORETTA YOUNG

MARLENE DIETRICH

By 1933, and from then on, The Crawford Look was making a big impression on women as her contemporaries, ladies of fashion and models all took on the Crawford style: eyes heavily lined and darkened, looking as huge as possible; the mouth enlarged into a Letty Lenton shape; the jaw square in a face with the bone structure emphasized; and of course, those large, square shoulders. It was a look that was to continue to dominate for succeeding decades, *de rigueur* for any beauty. Here are Adrienne Ames, Gertrude Michael, Marlene Dietrich, Marion Davies, Loretta Young and Dolores Del Rio.

DOLORES DEL RIO

CRAWFORD

Joan had been singing, sometimes very well, in nearly all of her thirties' films. *The Hollywood Revue* ("Gotta Feeling For You"), *Untamed* ("Chant of the Jungle"), *Montana Moon* ("The Moon Is Low"), *Laughing Sinners* ("What Can I Do—I Love That Man!"), *Possessed* ("How Long Will It Last?") led M-G-M to star her in the spectacular *Dancing Lady* in 1933. She went blonde again for this lavish musical, which co-starred Clark Gable and introduced both Fred Astaire and Nelson Eddy to the screen. The music was supplied by Rodgers and Hart, Jimmy McHugh and Dorothy Fields, Burton Lane and Harold Adamson, a stellar sextet indeed. Joan sang "Everything I Have Is Yours" cuddled in the arms of Franchot Tone, whom she soon married.

A series of painful teeth-cappings, necessary for the screen, considerably altered the shape of the mouth (helped by lipstick, of course) through the years. Here is Crawford, smiling, from *Rose Marie*, 1928, to *The Caretakers*, 1963. As the teeth got straighter and larger, the upper lip was pushed out and widened, which Crawford further exaggerates with makeup.

The late Douglass Montgomery told me that when he appeared opposite her in *Paid,* 1930, her mouth was so sore from the current teeth-capping that she had trouble eating, usually lunched on raisins, and then spent the rest of her lunch hour on interviews so she wouldn't feel the pain.

By strength of purpose and her own design, Crawford created
a face with the architectonic qualities of a head sculptured
by Phidias. Her bone structure was the delight of cameramen,
painters and sculptors.

325-65

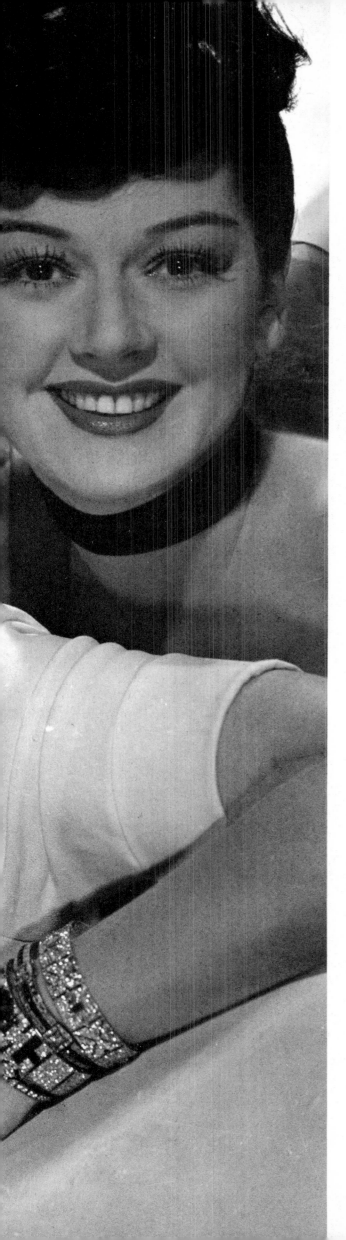

By 1939, Lucille LeSueur had been Billie Cassin, Mrs. Douglas Fairbanks, Jr., and Mrs. Franchot Tone. After her second divorce, and too long a period as a clothes horse in films with shallow plots, Crawford's career took an upward swing starting with *The Women*. Again imbued with a gnawing ambition to be a really fine actress, she played to the hilt the part of Crystal, a scheming, hard-boiled perfume clerk. Pitted against her in the all-woman cast were Norma Shearer, Rosalind Russell, Paulette Goddard, Joan Fontaine and Mary Boland, with Shearer and Russell her rivals in the picture.

It's interesting to note that all three ladies are wearing the large-mouth makeup popularized by Crawford. She had come a tremendous distance both career- and influence-wise in ten years since she appeared in *Our Modern Maidens,* in which Josephine Dunn and Anita Page were her rivals.

Crawford's resurgence after *The Women* was strengthened by three more fine
performances, which answered the questions that the fan magazines and some of the
critics had been asking, "Is Crawford Slipping?" "Are Joan's Screen-days Numbered?" etc.
A non-glamour part in *Strange Cargo* was followed by two brilliant performances, which
remain among her best, in *Susan and God* and *A Woman's Face*.

Of *Strange Cargo, Film Daily* wrote, "The acting is highgrade with Joan Crawford giving
her best performance to date." *Variety* dittoed, "Miss Crawford is provided with a
particularly meaty role . . . a departure from roles handed her during the past several years
[which] will give studio execs an idea of proper casting of her talents in the future." As
to *Susan and God, Variety* continued: "Joan Crawford provides a strong portrayal of Susan
. . . a marked departure for her. . . . The role provides the studio with a key to future
assignments for its star." Howard Barnes *(New York Herald-Tribune)* wrote, "Her characterization of Susan represents the best acting job she has done in a long time." The public
seemed to agree, and welcomed the sight of Crawford as an adult young woman playing roles
that were commensurate with her real age (36). Her dogged determination to be the first,
her unlimited capacity for hard work and, above all, her fantastic discipline had again
triumphed. The face took on an added strength and character.

The time from *The Gorgeous Hussy* to
A Woman's Face was only five years but the
years represented the advancement of a
young winner and champion to a distinguished performer who was at her peak. It
seems to me the whole story of that advancement is told here in the contrast between the
two large portraits. In 1936, she had refined
her face, eliminated the artificial exaggera-
tions of the early 30s. By 1941, her unusual
features had further mellowed into a thor-
oughbred face of authority and dignity, still
dramatic but under the control of her precise
purpose and will.

Study i

Part of the scope of Joan Crawford's amazing durability can be told in the list of the (screen) men in her life. In her first four years, she was leading lady to the top male stars on the lot, supporting Jackie Coogan, Harry Langdon, Charles Ray, Tim McCoy, Lon Chaney, John Gilbert, William Haines and Ramon Novarro. But after she became a star in *Our Modern Maidens* in 1929, she had a succession of leading men and co-stars unmatched by any other actress in the history of the screen.

Left:
1. With Robert Montgomery and William Powell
2. Clark Gable
3. Neil Hamilton
4. Robert Taylor

Above:
1. Spencer Tracy
2. Brian Aherne, Frank Morgan and Frank Conroy
3. Robert Young and Franchot Tone
4. Melvyn Douglas (Incidentally, Douglas is the only male star who played with all Four Fabulous Faces. He was with Swanson in *Tonight or Never*, with Garbo in *As You Desire Me, Ninotchka* and *Two-Faced Woman*, with Dietrich in *Angel*, and with Crawford in *The Shining Hour, A Woman's Face* and *They All Kissed the Bride*.)

Other men in her M-G-M life were: Johnny Mack Brown, Douglass Montgomery, Nils Asther, John Barrymore, Lionel Barrymore, William Gargan, Gary Cooper, Gene Raymond, Jimmy Stewart, Alan Curtis, Lew Ayres, Fredric March, Conrad Veidt, Herbert Marshall, John Wayne and Fred MacMurray.

Her second career, which began with *Mildred Pierce*, had playing opposite her: Jack Carson, Zachary Scott, John Garfield, Van Heflin, Raymond Massey, Dana Andrews, Jack Palance, Michael Wilding, Gig Young, Sterling Hayden, Jeff Chandler, Barry Sullivan, Cliff Robertson, Rossano Brazzi, Leif Erickson and John Ireland.

There is *no* other star, male or female, whose film career spans so many years (45) or so many films (80).

By 1942, Crawford, her public and the critics were growing increasingly unhappy with the pictures she was making. After her advancement with *The Women, Susan and God* and *A Woman's Face*, her next few films left a great deal to be desired.

"I wanted varied and challenging parts and instead got pictures that demanded nothing more than that I wear chic clothes. Pictures like *Random Harvest* and *Madam Curie* went to Greer Garson. If you think I made poor pictures after *A Woman's Face*, you should have seen the ones I went on suspension *not* to make," she has said.

So, after 18 years, she left M-G-M studios where "Joan Crawford" had been born. The war years created a need for something different in entertainment, and Crawford was determined to find it. It took her three long, difficult years.

The wistful girl on the left and the one below, who is having her fortune told by Minnie Flynn, both seem to be pondering her future, which in 1944 and 1945 didn't seem too promising. She was without a contract, had an unemployed young husband, Philip Terry, and two adopted children (twin daughters were to be adopted later). Terry went to work at an aircraft factory, the couple lost their cook to another defense factory and the children's nurse joined the WAVES. It was a time of victory gardens, helping out at the Hollywood Canteen, war work, with Joan alone taking care of her family and home. *Right:* with her son, Christopher, at the circus.

Two days after leaving M-G-M, she signed
a contract with Warner Brothers at a
third of what she had previously earned.
To her great credit, she refused to work until
she had a really good picture; so there was
a long, heartbreaking period of voluntary
retirement before she found that right script.
That script was *Mildred Pierce*, from the
tough James M. Cain novel. Bette Davis had
turned down the role. Warners wanted Ann
Sheridan, and director Michael Curtis preferred Barbara Stanwyck. But Crawford
(aided by producer Jerry Wald and agent
Lew Wasserman) fought for it and won it.
Her performance, with the familiar mannerisms subdued, was restrained but had depth
and dimension. It restored her not only to
stardom but also, to her great satisfaction, to
the position of actress, which was no surprise
to those who remembered her performances
at Metro when she had a good script and a
strong director. She had already showed that
she could tangle successfully with Hollywood's best in *Grand Hotel, The Women,
Susan and God* and *A Woman's Face*. (Sixteen years later, she was to take on her arch
rival, Bette Davis, in *Whatever Happened to
Baby Jane?* and to give, I think, the better
performance. Davis was marvelously spectacular but Crawford was so beautifully
suppressed with such inner strength in the
more difficult role that she won *my* vote.)

Crawford's spectacular comeback in Mildred
Pierce was sealed with the Academy Award
for best actress of 1945. She followed it with
a better performance in *Humoresque* (1946),
right, and an even better one in *Possessed,*
1947, winning another Academy Award
nomination.

658-178

During the 50s, Crawford made eleven films, including *Harriet Craig, Sudden Fear* (her third Academy Award nomination), *Torch Song* and *Autumn Leaves.* On May 9, 1955, she married Alfred N. Steel, president of Pepsi-Cola, and soon found that she'd wed not only a man but also his company. She became part of his world, traveling all over the globe with him on business for Pepsi-Cola. When Mr. Steel died in 1959, Crawford was elected to the board of Pepsi-Cola two days after his death, a position she has maintained ever since. She has done an outstanding job of merging actress with business woman and has made the names of Joan Crawford and Pepsi-Cola synonymous.

As the mouth increased in size, so did the eyes and eyebrows. Everthing about Crawford, her figure, her face, her hair, her mouth, her eyes and eyebrows, kept going through a continuing series of experiments and changes.

The change in eyebrows began in the 20s, plucked in the prevailing mode, rather straight and wistful above the eyes. For awhile, they became more natural, then altered to the pencil-thin style of the early 30s. By 1936, they had grown thicker and have continued to do so until, in the past decade, nourished by a mixture of castor oil and yellow Vaseline, they rival in glory those of Groucho Marx and John L. Lewis.

circa 1965

930

1933

1935

299

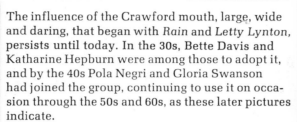

The influence of the Crawford mouth, large, wide and daring, that began with *Rain* and *Letty Lynton*, persists until today. In the 30s, Bette Davis and Katharine Hepburn were among those to adopt it, and by the 40s Pola Negri and Gloria Swanson had joined the group, continuing to use it on occasion through the 50s and 60s, as these later pictures indicate.

◀ Immediately following the death of her husband, Alfred Steel, Crawford was offered a part in *The Best of Everything* by old friend and producer Jerry Wald.

▼ In 1962, teaming with Bette Davis, she gave one of the best performances of her long career in *Whatever Happened to Baby Jane?* It revived her career and began a cycle of horror films that included *Strait Jacket*, 1964. ▲

▶ Off screen, she became a grandmother by son Christopher, and traveled the world more and more on behalf of Pepsi-Cola, maintaining an unusually disciplined social and business calendar.

Marlene Dietrich

VII

When Marlene Dietrich arrived in Hollywood in 1930 to make her first picture there, she came to a town in which the dust was still settling after a major upheaval in the motion picture industry—the advent of talking pictures. Old thrones in the motion picture industry had toppled, others were still shaky, and, in the aftermath, an entirely new group of performers was competing for audience approval.

It had all begun in 1927 when Warner Brothers, a minor-league studio that had little to lose and (as it turned out) everything to gain, decided to chance a device called Vitaphone, which was being offered by the Bell Telephone system. The major movie companies had already rejected it: they were too prosperous with their stables of money-making stars and chains of theaters to want to change. But Warner Brothers was not, and so the studio persuaded Al Jolson to accept stock in their company in lieu of salary to try a film using the new device. *The Jazz Singer,* with several songs and only a few lines of introductory dialogue, was released in October 1927. Although the picture itself was stilted and old-fashioned, audiences were fascinated by the new medium and box-office returns were sensational. The company quickly rushed out other films with increasing use of sound and by the spring of 1928, *any* sound picture—no matter how poor—would outdraw the best silent. Newsreels added sound, while short subjects gave vaudeville and stage performers the chance to be *heard* and seen. The major companies were forced into the realization that silent films were doomed and they must re-equip for the new medium, which already was proving fatal to many of their expensive contract players. Overnight, old-established favorites fell from popularity as their talkie debuts proved them inadequate and disenchanting, while even experienced stage stars suffered from the crudities of early sound recordings.

A critic wrote of John Gilbert, the classic case of the voice not fitting the visual personality, "It isn't that Mr. Gilbert's voice is insufficient; it's that his use of it robs him of magnetism, individuality, and, strangest of all, skill. He becomes an uninteresting and inexperienced performer whose work could be bettered by hundreds of lesser known players."

Other stars also could not master the new technique: Tom Mix, Corinne Griffith, Col-

leen Moore, Emil Jannings, Mae Murray and Vilma Banky were soon dropped by their studios. Still others were limited by their accents: the nasal Brooklyn twangs of Clara Bow and Norma Talmadge proved disillusioning: the latter's voice in her talkie performance in *DuBarry* caused the comment, "She speaks the Belascoan rodomontades in a Vitagraph accent." Miss Talmadge, wealthy and a bit bored with moviemaking anyway, decided to accept the advice of her sister, Constance, already retired, who wired her, "Leave them while you're looking good and thank God for the trust fund Mama set up." She was one of the fortunate few who were too old, too comfortable and too rich really to care, so they were able to take advantage of the huge salaries, low taxes, and wise investments which made "retirement" attractive. Hollywood supplanted them with new voices from the Broadway stage in ever-increasing numbers as the public showed its approval of Fredric March, Ann Harding, Claudette Colbert, Paul Muni, Miriam Hopkins, Clark Gable, Robert Montgomery, Irene Dunne, Spencer Tracy, Jeanette MacDonald and James Cagney.

For some inexplicable reason, at first foreign accents were considered unacceptable. I suppose the success of the "stage-English" voices of Ruth Chatterton, William Powell, Clive Brook, Leslie Howard, Jeanne Eagels and John Barrymore prompted the producers to assume that the public would not approve the accents of Emil Jannings and Pola Negri, for they were not even voice tested. Vilma Banky, Antonio Moreno, Karl Dane and Renee Adoree lost their contracts during this period of cultured tones and broad *a*'s. Fortunately, as recording techniques improved, a more natural mode of speaking gradually became accepted for performers whose voices reflected the image of their personalities.

Then, the almost simultaneous success of Garbo in *Anna Christie* and *Romance* and the debut of Dietrich in *Morocco* and *The Blue Angel* started another trend that reversed the old thinking. Audiences *would* accept an accent when the personality was strong enough, as in the cases of these two and of Chevalier. So Hollywood began again to import foreign talent like Charles Boyer, Anna Sten and Hedy LaMarr. But most of the early favorites previously mentioned never regained their former status even though subsequent films proved that many of them could speak and perform capably in talkies. At the time of Dietrich's importation, her new studio, Paramount, already had quite a galaxy of female stars for which it had to find suitable films.

The competition was keen, with Ruth Chatterton and Nancy Carroll leading the list, while coming up quickly in the box-office sweepstakes were Sylvia Sidney, Kay Francis, Claudette Colbert, Jeanette MacDonald, Miriam Hopkins and Carole Lombard. Tallulah Bankhead was brought back from England but somehow her vivid personality seemed too esoteric for the Depression-era audiences. The condition was eased a bit when Chatterton and Kay Francis left Paramount to join Warner Brothers in 1932, but by that time, Mae West had arrived on the lot to even the score. I mention all of this because the immediate success of Dietrich becomes all the more remarkable when the circumstances of it are called to mind.

The situation was equally crowded at other studios: M-G-M had Crawford, Garbo, Harlow, Shearer, Myrna Loy, Marion Davies and Helen Hayes, while soon to come were Luise Rainer, Hedy LaMarr and Rosalind Russell. Among the other top favorites of the early 30s were such holdovers from silents as Gloria Swanson, Bebe Daniels, Loretta Young, Janet Gaynor and Dolores Del Rio. And there were Ann Harding, Barbara Stanwyck, Irene Dunne, Joan and Constance Bennett, and Katharine Hepburn—plus the fast-rising Ginger Rogers, Jean Arthur, Ruby Keeler, Margaret Sullavan, Merle Oberon and Ann Sothern. Elissa Landi, Lili Damita, Anna Sten, and Madeleine Carroll were imported for their day in the sun. It's a bit overwhelming when one thinks of this profusion of ladies, all competing for audience favor to achieve and retain star status. What a contrast to the paucity of top women stars in the cinema world today.

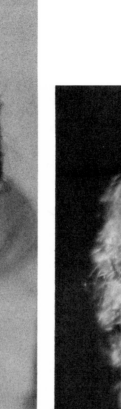

JOAN BENNETT

NORMA SHEARER

DOLORES COSTELLO   BEBE DANIELS   MARION DAVIES

CAROLE LOMBARD   JEAN ARTHUR   ANN SOTHERN

ANN HARDING   KATHARINE HEPBURN   ANNA STEN

MIRIAM HOPKINS

KAY FRANCIS

RUTH CHATTERTON

CONSTANCE BENNETT

DOLORES DEL RIO

LILI DAMITA

MAE WEST

MYRNA LOY

DIETRICH

On these first few pages is the young Dietrich of German theater and films before *The Blue Angel* catapulted her overnight into international fame. This group of pictures shows her from 1927 through 1929 and refutes, I think, the now accepted legend that she was then a heavy, overweight woman who could not be photographed properly. Although she *is* heavier in some pictures than she was to become in America, in the others she looks quite slim and lovely.

During the late 20s, she was appearing successfully on the Berlin stage in a popular revue in 1926 called *It's in the Air,* and in a Max Reinhardt version of the Broadway success, *Broadway.* In 1927, she made her first records,

phot. Willinger.

two of which, "Peter" and "Jonny," have remained part of her vocal repertoire. Her films included *Manon Lescaut, A Modern DuBarry* and *Heads up, Charly* in 1926; *The Imaginary Baron, His Greatest Bluff,* and *Cafe Electric* in 1927; *Princess Olala,* (while, on stage, she appeared in Shaw's *Misalliance* and *Two Neckties*) in 1928; she filmed *I Kiss Your Hand, Madame, The Woman One Longs for, The Ship of Lost Souls,* and *Gefahren der Brautzeit* in 1929.

Marlene Dietrich

It was while appearing in the play, *Two Neckties*, in Berlin, 1929, that Josef Von Sternberg first saw her and picked her for the film he had come from America to direct, *The Blue Angel*. Emil Jannings was the star but today the unique distinction of the film is Dietrich and the aura extended by her performance. When James Joyce, some years later, told Dietrich that he had seen her in *The Blue Angel,* she replied, ''Then, Monsieur, you have seen the best of me.''

On Stage: Marlene and Eric Odemor in Shaw's *Misalliance,* directed by Max Reinhardt at the Deutsche Theatre, 1928. In Films: *Sein Grosster Bluff* (His Greatest Bluff), 1927, starring Harry Piel (the Douglas Fairbanks of Germany), who also directed it. Her suggestive, monocled smile already hints at the fascinating ambiguity soon to become part of the legend.

The Blue Angel, with its consummate decadence and stunning, perverse visual effects, usually appears on every critic's list of all-time best films. This mordant work of cinema art, originally released in the U.S. in 1930, contained the talkie debut of Emil Jannings who had been one of the great silent stars in both German and American films, and was filmed simultaneously in English and in German. In it, Dietrich scored a personal success unmatched by any other actress: she became the first film performer to become a star on the strength of just one film, a film that today is chiefly associated with the woman who became one of the greatest superstars that the screen ever produced.

Her subtly corrosive cabaret singer, Lola-Lola, remains the prototype of all the screen's faithless floozies.

Right: This portrait was taken in New York by Irving Chidnoff in 1930 when she was en route to Hollywood to make her first film there. The marvelous bone structure, molded cheekbones and high forehead were all there—ready for the ensuing changes to be wrought by Josef Von Sternberg in his magically beautiful films. The process starts on the following pages.

You may have noticed that in these early Hollywood portraits Dietrich does not resemble the face that soon was to rock the world. As she and Von Sternberg searched every lighting possibility best to present her, she was lit in a variety of ways: from the right, from the left, or silhouetted from behind, thus achieving a variety of looks. She is incredibly beautiful in all of them but the denouement was yet to come.

Notice (here and later on) the cigarette that was soon to become such a trademark, a Dietrich specialty out of which she made an art.

Dietrich's hair had a lot of red in it, making it photograph darker than it actually was. Its color gradually became more gold (in fact, for awhile, she used an unbelievably expensive gold dust on it for highlight) until she finally settled on the blonde shade we know today.

When overhead lighting produced the fabulous
result above, illuminating the sculptured look of her
bone structure, Dietrich insisted that it be kept from
then on. It gave her a unique quality, a refined
modeling that the beautiful face on the left lacked.
Just a key-light above in front, casting a downward
light, and sometimes another light in back to
silhouette the hair, produces the results that the
world knows so well—the prominent cheekbones,
well-modeled nose, deep-set eyes and soft
sensual lips.

Two portraits from *Dishonored,* the second U.S. film in which her face, bathed in soft shadows, constantly took on new forms and contours. In it, she wore the extraordinary Hermes Kit black chain outfit, seen left.

Of her performance in *Dishonored,* Richard A. Watts, Jr., wrote: "She proves once more that her hasty rise to film celebrity was the result of neither luck, accident, nor publicity....Her almost lyrically ironic air of detachment and, to be as frank about it as possible, her physical appeal, make her one of the great personages of the local drama."

The by now recurring phrase, "and Miss Dietrich has never looked so beautiful," was certainly indisputably true of her in *Shanghai Express,* which won an Academy Award for its photography. With her eyebrows plucked and penciled into a new, butterfly-wing arrangement, Dietrich was shadowed, furred and feathered, a phantom houri with a panoply of wonder, moistened lips and dewy eyes.

With this film, Dietrich put a finalization to the Garbo-Dietrich comparison: she was so utterly unique, so completely her own personality, that her fans and imitators became legion. Her poetic, chiaroscuric films were escapist fare for a Depression audience. The Parisian fashion and art worlds were captivated to the extent that one's status depended on the number of times one had seen her in *Shanghai Express:* artist Christian Bérard claimed to be the winner with an attendance record of 38 times. It is in this film that the immortal line, "It took more than one man to change my name to Shanghai Lily" is uttered by Dietrich to Clive Brook, who reacts to this revelation with a stoic impassiveness that an oriental diplomat might well envy.

◄ *Blonde Venus* provided Marlene with the memorable musical cantata "Hot Voodoo." She appears first encased in a giant gorilla disguise, flanked by dancing native girls; then, emerging from this startling armor, she dons a fuzzy white wig to sing her provocative song to a very young Cary Grant.

Josef Von Sternberg was Dietrich's director, advisor and mentor during her first six years in Hollywood and remained her good friend until his death, December 22, 1969. In her book, *Marlene Dietrich's ABC,* she describes him simply as "the man I wanted to please most." Their collaboration was thought of as a strange Svengali-Trilby relationship by many because Dietrich, who was imperious and temperamental in her relations with others, was passive, pliant and submissive to his every demand, never complaining or questioning the long, grueling hours he kept her working.

Von Sternberg had a genius for conveying the essence of enchantment as a power of selective rather than exhaustive detail. The resplendent tapestries of the films he created for her were so intricately woven that the amazing economy of his *mise en scène* was often overlooked; for example, he would suggest a crowded ballroom scene with a minimum of extras, some balloons and confetti floating through the air.

Dietrich refutes the suggestion that she, too, was only a thread in the design of his films, saying that he created "camera vehicles...done with imagery...that was the meaning and purpose of his pictorialism. He taught me that the image of a screen character is built not alone from her acting and appearance but out of everything that is cumulatively visible in a film. He taught me about camera angles, lighting, costumes, makeup, timing, matching scenes, cutting and editing...the most creative experience I ever had."

In 1932, when *Blonde Venus* was released, mother love, forced to parade down Sin Street for the sake of son and sustenance, was a theme prescribed for most of the top cinema ladies. Dietrich, Constance Bennett, Tallulah Bankhead, Ruth Chatterton and even Garbo made the sordid self-sacrifice required by Depression soap-operas.
◄ The young housewife and loving mother seen at the beginning of the film, a bunch of violets clasped to her apron.
► A Galveston, Texas, skid row is now the background for Dietrich, playing a streetwalker with only a cigarette to sustain her.

Dietrich's 1933 production, *Song of Songs,* was a talkie version of the 1924 Pola Negri silent, *Lily of the Dust.* Adapted from the novel by Hermann Sudermann and directed by Rouben Mamoulian, it was Dietrich's first U.S. film not under the guidance of Von Sternberg. A visual treat, sumptuously staged, it had a dull, dated story that was notable for scenes in which Dietrich posed nude for a life-size statue sculpted by Brian Aherne (making his U.S. film debut), and for Dietrich's singing of her early German recording hit, "Jonny," with new lyrics in English written by Eddie Heyman. In her theater tours of the past decades, "Jonny" has been an important song in the Dietrich repertoire, but for some inexplicable reason, she always has sung it in German "because the English words were never written for it," an announcement that lyricist Heyman must ponder in his grave.

The red-gold hair of former years is now entirely blonde and has usually remained that shade ever since, except for a technicolor opus, *The Garden of Allah.* The mouth is fuller while the extended butterfly's antenna eyebrows of *Shanghai Express* have resumed a more normal position.

Here are portraits of Dietrich in *The Scarlet Empress,* surely one of the most spectacular, stupefyingly sensual films ever conceived. Delight Evans, in her *Screenland* review wrote: "Josef Von Sternberg, supreme stylist of the screen, presents his most lavish and fantastic production. It's overpowering, unreal, bizarre, but it is so opulently eyefilling, so gorgeous in its pageantry, so exquisitely photographed that I wouldn't miss it if I were you.... Dietrich, never more beautiful, makes the transition from gauche childhood to disillusioned womanhood with exquisite understanding.... [Her] closeups in candle-light and in veils, large as life, and twice as lovely, are amazing.... The grotesque images which abound amused me mightily and I do not agree with most critics that they dwarf the characters. Let Mr. Von Sternberg have his little joke. His highly developed sense of beauty and satire more than atone."

Cecilia Ager's brilliant description of
Dietrich in *The Devil Is a Woman*
(*Variety*, May 8, 1935) can hardly be
improved upon: "Not even Garbo in the
Orient [Ed. note—*The Painted Veil*] has
approached, for spectacular effects,
Dietrich in Spain. With fringes, lace,
sequins, carnations, chenille, nets,
embroideries and shawls, Miss Dietrich is
hung, wrapped, draped, swathed and
festooned...her costumes are magnificent
in the way they achieve a definite,
clear-cut line despite their wealth of
ornature, the way their knick-knacks fall
into a pattern designed with flair and
imagination solely to flatter and adorn.
Her costumes are completely incredible,
but completely fascinating and suitable to
The Devil Is a Woman. They reek with
glamour."
(All of Dietrich's clothes in her Paramount
films were designed by Travis Banton.
He dressed a long list of stars that
included Carole Lombard, Mae West,
Claudette Colbert and Miriam Hopkins,
but Dietrich was his favorite, and for her
he always outdid himself.)

Miss Ager's description continued: "Miss Dietrich's mask-like makeup and bizarre coiffures abound with beauty hints. When she lowers her shiny, heavy eyelids, it may be seen that eyelashes are affixed only to the outer halves of her upper eyelids, intensifying thus the wide-spacing of her eyes and yielding them a provocative upward slant. Her lower lids are deliberately not accented with black, which would define the boundaries of her eyes and so limit their size. Her natural eyebrows have been blotted out and soaring new ones etched far above. . . . Though her head is bedecked with an infinite variety of Spanish combs, flowers, shawls, fringes and veils, they've been arranged so as to frame her face, never to intrude their fripperies upon its expertly enhanced, submissive beauty. Miss Dietrich emerges as a glorious achievement, a supreme consolidation of the sartorial, makeup and photographic arts."

Although it was probably her least successful film, Dietrich chose it as her favorite. "I was more beautiful in that than in anything else" (*Life,* August 18, 1952). Having seen the film four times in the past four years, I can agree. Her performance is one of my favorites: never has she played more tongue-in-cheek, more camp, or with more joy and abandon in a role. The style of her performance in this picture was full of wit and dizzy contradictions, displaying a disciplined control of high parody. It gave more than a hint of the performance that she was to essay with such success four years later in *Destry Rides Again.*

New York City, circa 1950
Marlene and Maria: Germany, 1930
Hollywood, 1934

When Dietrich first came to the United States alone, she spoke proudly of her young daughter, Maria, whipping out a picture of her on the least pretext. Returning from Germany in 1931, she brought her daughter and husband Rudolph Sieber with her to Hollywood and allowed Maria to play the role of the child Catherine in *The Scarlet Empress*. Maria was raised in the United States, although a kidnap scare resulted in her going to school in Switzerland for awhile. In the early 50s, she had a successful acting career on TV in New York City, where she met and married William Riva, and now lives in Paris with her husband and four sons.

ANNA STEN

Just as in the case of the other three Fabulous Faces, Dietrich exerted a tremendous influence on the change in appearance and physiognomy of screen glamour from the 30s to the present. After her phenomenal success, each studio tried for a Dietrich of its own, and there soon appeared a succession of browless, languid ladies, all of them hollow-cheeked creatures seen through filters of cigarette smoke and shadows, who spoke and sang in a variety of accents. Several excellent Continental actresses, Anna Sten, Isa Miranda, and Lil Dagover, were sacrificed on the altar of imitation. None of the pseudo-Dietrichs could match the style or appeal of the original, even though her lighting, makeup, hair and clothes were studiously copied. American girls were also influenced: by 1933 no self-respecting beauty was photographed without deep hollows in her cheeks and seductive shadows on her face. Left is Anna Sten, and Tallulah Bankhead (with Paul Lucas) in *Thunder Below,* ▼ and opposite, reading clockwise, Carole Lombard, Alice Faye, Lana Turner, Marilyn Monroe and Gwili Andre carrying on the Dietrich tradition from the 30s through the 60s.

TALLULAH BANKHEAD

CAROLE LOMBARD

ALICE FAYE

LANA TURNER

GWILI ANDRE

MARILYN MONROE

Social Life In Holywood in the 30s.
Carole Lombard gave a Coney Island-type
party at the Santa Monica pier where the
guests, dressed informally, rode the roller
coasters and whooped it up just like
common folk.
◄ Carole, Cary Grant, Dietrich and Richard
Barthelmess.
► Dietrich and William Haines
▼ With Clifton Webb and Elizabeth Allan
(who came dressed as Dietrich) at a costume
party given by the Basil Rathbones.
Dietrich, as Leda and the Swan, was a
sensation—with every feather on her
costume dyed the exact shade of blue
matching her eyes. Hedda Hopper told me
that she spent two days with the designers
seeing that *every* feather was perfectly
placed.

Off Stage

► Dietrich with Felix Rolo and Princess
Natalie Paley (Mrs. John Wilson).

Douglas Fairbanks, Jr.

John Gilbert

Jean Gabin

Brian Aherne ►

MARLENE DIETRICH
in Paramount Pictures

351

The mouth and eyebrows go through quite a metamorphosis of their own during three decades.

◄ "I am, at heart, a gentleman," she once
told a friend. This early photograph is from
the cabaret scene in *Morocco,* 1930. In
Blonde Venus, she wore a silver top hat and
tails; in *Seven Sinners,* a navy uniform; in
Rancho Notorious, cowboy clothes; and,
for the first few years of her nightclub and
theater act, she appeared in the second act
wearing black or white top hat and tails.
▲ At her most feminine. A candid
snapshot on the set of *Angel,* 1937, by
Hymie Fink, who said of it, "The most
beautiful grab-shot I've ever taken."

The portrait (of the braided, peasant girl)
is a rare one from an abandoned, aborted
film variously called *Hotel Imperial,
Invitation to Happiness* and *I Loved a
Soldier*. It was to have been a remake
of one of Pola Negri's finest silents,
which had been directed by Maurice
Stiller, Garbo's Swedish director.
This version had Charles Boyer as co-star,
but disaster overtook it so finally it was
shelved and the cost, $900,000, written off.
(Shades of Gloria Swanson in *Queen
Kelly!*) Co-star Boyer rejoined Dietrich in
her next film, *The Garden of Allah*.

1356-167

Some of her co-stars and leading men included: *left:* Clive Brook in *Shanghai Express; above left:* John Lund in *A Foreign Affair; above right:* Melvyn Douglas in *Angel;* and *below:* Gary Cooper in *Morocco.* Others included Victor McLaglen, Herbert Marshall, Cary Grant, Brian Aherne, Cesar Romero, Charles Boyer, Robert Donat, Jimmy Stewart, John Wayne, Randolph Scott, Bruce Cabot, Edward G. Robinson, George Raft, Fred MacMurray, Orson Welles, Ronald Colman, Jean Gabin, Ray Milland, Michael Wilding, Richard Todd, Mel Ferrer, Vittorio De Sica, Tyrone Power, Charles Laughton and Spencer Tracy. Sounds like a roll call of the best that Hollywood could offer for 40 years, doesn't it!

Marlene's magical, marvelous legs have been an object of admiration since she first strutted out on stage to straddle a chair and sing her immortal "Falling in Love Again" in *The Blue Angel.* Here she and they are seen in scenes from *Morocco*, left, and *Song of Songs*, below.
Across the page: "Marlene relaxing in her garden" and poses from *The Devil Is a Woman,* and *Kismet,* in which her legs were painted gold.

The gorgeous gams are seen here in poses from *Morocco, Manpower, No Highway in the Sky* and *Destry Rides Again.* Not only her legs, but also her subtle and expressive use of her hands, arms and entire body to convey meaning and evoke emotion seems remarkably outstanding to me. "She handles her body like Stradivarius used to handle his violins. And no matter what kind of finish it happens to be wearing at the time, it is still a masterpiece" (attributed to John Barrymore).

Other top stars and beauties in the middle 30s and early 40s included:
Top: JEAN HARLOW, MYRNA LOY, CLAUDETTE COLBERT
Middle: MARIA MONTEZ, CONSTANCE MOORE, DOLORES DEL RIO
Bottom: ALICE FAYE, JESSIE MATTHEWS, IRENE DUNNE
(Right Page): DOROTHY LAMOUR, JEANETTE MACDONALD, ILONA
MASSEY, HEDY LAMARR

1942

1935

Looking at portraits like these, one can readily perceive why Dietrich has been called "a photographer's dream." She is *sui generis*.

Dietrich, along with Crawford, Hepburn, Astaire and Mae West, was declared "box-office poison" by not very astute exhibitors in 1937. She was off the screen for nearly two years until her triumphant "comeback" in *Destry Rides Again,* 1939. In it and in her next film, *Seven Sinners,* she gave two of her best and most popular performances. Howard Barnes, *New York Herald-Tribune,* wrote: "Marlene Dietrich comes into her own again in *Seven Sinners....* Here you will find the tough, glamorous, eloquent demi-mondaine of *The Blue Angel.* If anything, she is even better than she was in that original triumph.... She cuts loose with a perfect impersonation of a high-class slattern. It's a fine performance in a stunning, romantic melodrama."

Ray Jones, who took the large portrait on the next page, said, "What Monroe is to sex, Dietrich is to glamour. With that woman, just one light—and a photographer has a priceless piece of sculpture. The high forehead, the arch between the eyes, those soft lips slightly parted...what a sight."

1083-57

1083-20

Could anyone look more magical, more marvelous, more magnificent in period costumes than Marlene, the most modern of women?

Flame of New Orleans ▲

◄ *The Spoilers, 1942* ▼ *Rancho Notorious, 1952*

"The Art of the Cigarette"—
No one else was ever able to make such a specialty, such a co-star of an object as Dietrich did with a cigarette. Next time you go through the Dietrich section of this book, notice her skillful mastery of it, count the innumerable ways she has of handling it—making the prop an integral and indispensable part of the whole picture. Her contemporaries were well aware of this asset. *Above:* Our old friend, Pola Negri, in blonde wig with cigarette in the German-made *Mazurka Tragica,* 1935.

In 1944, Louis Kronenberger in *P.M.* wrote: "After *Kismet*, God had better give up trying to compete with M-G-M." Dietrich's legs were painted gold for this film, and she made another *Life* cover showing them thus adorned.
Far left: Dietrich in the Dior dress that she wore to the Academy Award presentation, 1949.

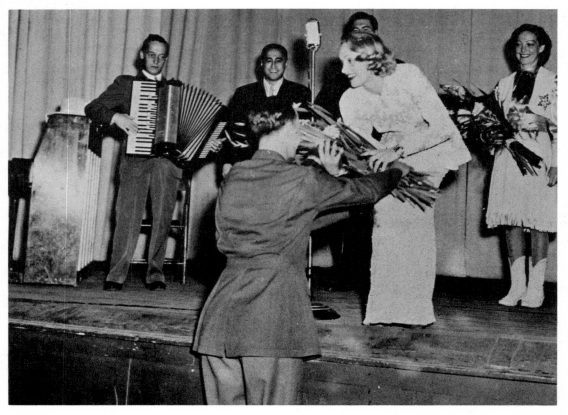

Dietrich joined the U.S.O. in 1943 to tour overseas for the next three years, for which she was awarded the Medal of Freedom by General Maxwell D. Taylor.
Above: Washing her face in the snow, Malmédy, Belgium.
Below: Her U.S.O. camp show in Iceland.
Above: Her first U.S. film after the war was *Golden Earrings,* 1947.
Right: In 1950, she made *Stage Fright* in England for Alfred Hitchcock. Her friend, Noel Coward, said, "She may be the greatest woman of our age...but so damned intelligent for a woman."

Above: A Foreign Affair, 1948, was one of Dietrich's biggest hits and most critical
successes. *Life* magazine said, "As a singer in the nightclub, Dietrich enjoys a return
to the sexy role that made her famous eighteen years ago in the German film,
The Blue Angel."
Left: A portrait from *The Monte Carlo Story,* 1957.

Touring the world with her nightclub act, she traveled to South America, England, Scotland, France, Holland, Israel, Germany, Canada, South Africa, Australia and Russia.

Judgement at Nuremberg, 1961.

For the past few decades, Dietrich has toured the world with her unique and successful one-woman stage performance. Wisely, she limits the number of engagements each year to an amount which doesn't tire her nor exhaust the interest of her audiences.

It is doubtful that she will ever make another film since roles that she considers appropriate seem scarce. For years, she flirted with the idea of a Dietrich Television Special and wanted Orson Welles to produce and direct it, but somehow that concept never materialized. Finally, in 1972, she did appear in a two-hour TV Special in London which was shortened to less than an hour for American audiences.

When she isn't traveling for her performances, most of her time is spent in Paris to be near her daughter Maria, who lives there with her husband and four sons. Dietrich keeps another apartment in New York City but is there so seldom that it is usually sublet.

Like the three other Faces, she persists as an outstanding symbol and image of glamour and professional perfection. Too, there remains the marvelous legacy of her films from Hollywood's Golden Age plus her recordings and stage performances, all of which continue to enchant and to create new fans and audiences. Today's young people seem just as enthralled as were those who saw her in the 30's, 40's and 50's.

Her one-woman theater act has captured the enthusiastic approbation of audiences all over the world. The flesh-colored chiffon gown by Jean-Louis, covered with rhinestones and sequins, is a part of the polish and perfection that they see and applaud, as smoothly, effortlessly, she wraps them around her little finger.

This color section begins with an original painting by Henry Clive of Gloria Swanson, *opposite.* Mr. Clive was a leading artist whose covers appeared on the old *Smart Set,* which was edited by H. L. Mencken and George Jean Nathan, and on *Picture Play* and *Screen Book.* The section also has some rare color photographs.

But it is comprised mainly of paintings of the Four Fabulous Faces that appeared on the covers of magazines during the 20s and 30s, when the top commercial artists of those decades were painting the portraits seen here. At that time all magazines used paintings on their covers, and drawings for story illustrations in each issue until color photography usurped that function.

Periodicals vied with one another to obtain the services of the best artists available since the cover contributed strongly to the look and personality of the magazine and usually had a great deal to do with influencing a prospective reader to buy it. Covers also served another important purpose: the same artist's work seen every month year after year was a means of immediate identification for the reader. Seeing a Norman Rockwell cover meant the *Saturday Evening Post,* for example; a Harrison Fisher meant *Cosmopolitan;* Rolf Armstrong meant *College Humor;* and Earl Christy meant *Redbook.*

These cover artists earned deservedly lucrative sums for their paintings which, in their own way, were an *art nouveau* form that is lost today. Some of them combined the pastel freedom of Toulouse-Lautrec or Degas with the sweeping technique of Boldini or Sargent. Their work was vivid and meant to catch the eye, and it certainly did, as you'll see when you look at the many examples shown here.

Nearly all the artists worked in New York City where the magazines were published and so their color paintings of Hollywood stars usually were copied from photographs. Top stars like these four might appear on several covers a month, and they hardly had time to sit for artists that often. Sometimes the painters made an exact translation of the photograph to canvas but more often they used their imagination to transform their paintings into color portraits that were highly stylized and very individual. A study of the layouts illustrates various ways in which the artists interpreted the same photograph and provides a fascinating example of the difference in their conception, color and style.

Here are the covers of James Montgomery Flagg, McClelland Barclay, Hal Phyfe, Rolf Armstrong, Charles Sheldon, Earl Christy, Henry Clive, Martha Sawyers, Penrhyn Stanlaws, Modest Stein, Thomas Webb, Marland Stone, John Ralston Clark, Zoe Mozert, E. Dahl, Jay Weaver, Morr Kusnet, Jules Erbit, Jose M. Recoder, Irving Sinclair and Victor Tchetchet. Other prominent names appearing on cinema covers were those of Neisa McMein and Alfred Cheney Johnson for *Photoplay,* and Alberto Vargas (now known simply as Varga—of *Playboy* and *Esquire* fame), who painted for *Motion Picture* magazine. John Held, Jr., did covers and cartoons for *Screenland* in 1923, and W. T. Benda, famed for his bizarre and striking masks, for *Talking Pictures* magazine in 1930.

The quality of movie or fan magazines in the 20s and 30s is a startling contrast to that of the current crop. They were edited by knowledgeable people of taste and imagination who had great enthusiasm for the art of the motion picture and its people. Editors like James Quirk, Ernest V. Heyn, Delight Evans, Ruth Waterbury, Adela Rogers St. Johns, James Fredrick Smith, Katherine Albert and Eugene Brewster respected the intelligence and alertness of their readers. The staff of *Photoplay* in 1922 included Robert E. Sherwood, Ralph Barton, Margaret E. Sangeter, Willard Huntington Wright (S. S. Van Dine, Adela Rogers St. Johns, Burns Mantle and Terry Ramsage, who wrote the illustrious *The Romantic History of the Motion Picture.* Also writing for it that year were Anita Loos, Will Rogers, Channing Pollack, Mary Roberts Rhinehart, and Howard Dietz of Schwartz and Dietz song-writing fame.

Its contemporary, *Screenland,* in 1923, had George Jean Nathan for its drama critic, and stories by Elinor Glyn, Jim Tully, Upton Sinclair and Rupert Hughes. Featured cartoons were by men of the caliber of Covarrubias (whose work appeared also in *Vanity Fair),* Rube Goldberg and John Held, Jr., whose pert flappers were the personification of an era.

The first fan magazine was *Motion Picture,* founded in 1911. Its publisher soon added *Classic,* devoted to stage and screen, to the roster; *Classic* later became *Motion Picture Classic* in the mid-20s and *Movie Classic* in the 30s. The list of authors who wrote for *Motion Picture* and *Motion Picture Classic* in the 20s is pretty impressive: authors like W. Somerset Maugham, Joseph Hergesheimer Sir Arthur Conan Doyle. Thomas Burke, Rebecca West, Rex Beach, Al Smith, H. L. Mencken, A. A. Milne, Sir Anthony Hope, Vincente Blasco Ibáñez, Clarence Darrow Rupert Hughes and Herbert Hoover.

In the 20s, the movies were a new art form that intrigued the imagination of the top artists, writers and craftsmen in the world, and the magazines devoted to them drew on the best mine of talent extant to work for them. Beside top writers, renowned photographers like Cecil Beaton, Arnold Genthe, Hal Phyfe, Alfred Cheney Johnson, Nicholas Muray and Maurice Goldberg had their portraits in them, while famed cartoonists like John Decker, John Held, Jr., Leo Kober, Covarrubias and Wynn adorned their pages.

Delight Evans, upon becoming editor of *Screenland* in 1929, immediately declared that she wanted it to be worthy of residing next to *Vanity Fair* on the coffee table. She had George Gershwin and Oscar Strauss write articles on music, Molyneux and Chanel discussed clothes, Louis Bromfield, Edgar Wallace and J. P. McAvoy wrote articles. She hired Cecil Beaton from *Vanity Fair* for his essays and photographs, and inaugurated the first monthly column in a film magazine on radio.

In the Depression days of the 30s, new fan magazines tha sold for just 10¢ were originated to keep pace with the new talking screen. The *New Movie* magazine had Theodore Dreiser, Heywood Broun, Frank Sullivan, Cornelius Vanderbilt, Jr., Fanny Hurst, Anita Loos, Edwin C. Hill, O. O. McIntyre, Elsie Janis and Grand Duke Alexander of Russia as contributors. The renowned astrologist, Evangeline Adams, did a monthly column. *Modern Screen,* edited by Ernest V. Heyn, engaged Mrs. Franklin D. Roosevelt, Booth Tarkington, Irvin S. Cobb, Vicki Baum (author of *Grand Hotel),* Faith Baldwin Elinor Glyn, Nina Wilcox Putnam and artist Russell Patterson to write articles. In 1937, Heyn became executive editor of *Photoplay,* which, by then, was owned by Macfadden Publications. With Ruth Waterbury as editor, he enlarged *Photoplay* to the size of *Life* and *Look* and made it "The Aristocrat of Motion Picture magazines." Aimed at a class of readers who "buys the latest books, speaks accurately of current events, and knows the newest distance between a hemline and the floor," *Photoplay* in the next few years presented such writers as James Hilton, Rachel Field, Eleanor Roosevelt, Max Brand, John Erskine Louis Bromfield, Gilbert Seldes, Elsa Maxwell, Lloyd C. Douglas, Erle Stanley Gardner and the illustrations of artists Bradshaw Crandell, Charles D. Mitchell, McClellan Barclay, Neysa McMein, Vincentini, James Montgomery Flagg, Wallace Morgan and Russell Patterson.

Yesterday's film magazines were different from anything to be seen today, as inimitable as the industry and the people to whom they were devoted.

CLASSIC
PICTORIAL of SCREEN AND STAGE

A BREWSTER PUB

MOTION PICTVRE
THE QUALITY MAGAZINE OF THE SCREEN

NOVEMBER '23

MAGAZI
25 CTS

Gloria Swanson

IS A STAR GOOD FOR
ONLY THREE YEARS? See page 39.

MOTION PICTURE

NOVEMBER — 1 Shilling *1926*

HAT
O
EN
NT?

Why Do
Society Girls
Fail in
the Movies?

*Do You
Believe in
Haunted Houses?*
See Page 19

The National Guide to Motion Pictures

PHOTOPLAY

SEPTEMBER   25 CENTS

*Gloria
Swanson*

Why Mary Pickford
Bobbed Her Hair *In This*
Issue

PICTURE PLAY

25 cts.

DECEMBER 1929

STREET AND SMITH

Gloria Swanson
Painted by
MODEST STEIN

Stingy Stars of Hollywood

America's Smart Screen Magazine

SCREENLAND

FEB

Gloria
Swanson

Rolf Armstrong's
16 Screen Beauties

Edgar Wallace

394

movie
MIRROR

RUTH WATERBURY, EDITOR
JUNE *1933*

10¢

AN CRAWFORD
Sketched By
MONTGOMERY FLAGG

MOTION
PICTURE

ns

NOW
10¢
in Canada

MARCH

JOAN
CRAWFORD

**CORNELIUS
VANDERBILT, JR.
COVERS HOLLYWOOD**

HEPBURN IS SHY...SAYS NINA WILCOX PUTNAM

PHOTOPLAY

OCTOBER   25 CENTS

WHY MALE STARS
MARRY PLAIN GIRLS

JOAN
CRAWFORD
BY
TCHETCHET

movie
MIRROR

RUTH WATERBURY

10¢
A MACFADDEN
PUBLICATION

JUNE

NRA
WE DO OUR PART

Jo
CRAW

"The TRUTH about MYSELF and FRANCHOT TO
Revealed By JOAN CRAWFORD

SCREEN BOOK
MAGAZINE

10c

AUGUST

Joan Crawford

My Love Affair
with Constance Bennett
by -?

MARTHA SAWYER

The Smart Screen Magazine

SCREENLAND

July

NOW
15c
20c in Canada

Joan Crawford

WHAT *does the* FUTURE *hold for* GARBO

Hollywood's Own Moral Code

good

1931

THE NEW

SCREENLAND

The
SMART
SCREEN
MAGAZINE

March
25c

Marlene Dietrich

DIETRICH'S
SHADOW on
GARBO'S PATH**!**

Beginning
**MARIE
DRESSLER'S**
OWN STORY

PHOTOPLAY

MAY

25 CENT

Mary Pickford
on Facing Forty

How Norma Shea
Got What She Wan

NEW MOVIE MAGAZINE

10¢ IN U.S.
15 CENTS IN CANADA

MAY 1931

"THEY SAY.."

EXPOSING THE WHISPERING CHORUS

Win a trip to Hollywood! Fifty Prizes! See Page

A FAWCETT PUBLICATION

SCREEN PLAY

SECRETS OF HOLLYWOOD

JULY 25c

MARLENE DIETRICH BY HENRY CLIVE

The Girl Who Dared to Shoo the World

SCREEN BOOK
MAGAZINE

JUNE

10c

Marlene Dietrich

JOAN
CRAWFORD'S
STRANGE
ADVENTURE

THE AMAZING CASE
OF SALLY EILERS

Jose M. Recoder

REFLECTING the MAGIC of HOLLYWOOD
Silver Screen

10¢

SEPTEMBER

MARLENE
DIETRICH

The
ELEVEN
GENTLEMEN of
HOLLYWOOD

The
Unknown
Ruth
Chatterton

True Confessions

Fawcett's Magazine

MAY 25¢

Is My Daughter Safe?

Revelations of a Flapper's Mother

CLASSIC

FEBRUARY 25¢

Herges
Defe
Holly

Greta Ga

The Truth About Camera Angle

Motion Picture

DECEMBER

25 CENTS

Greta Garbo

MERLARD STONE

The Romance *of the Movies* --*By Benj. B. Hampton*
Babies For Sale --*Hollywood's Youngest Extras*

SCREENLAND

NOVEMBER

GRETA GARBO

Psycho-analyzed

SCREENLAND

JUNE
25c

THOMAE WEBB

Greta Garbo

A NEW SLANT ON GARBO!

Is Hollywood a Godless Town?

SCREENLAND

FEBRUARY, 1927

PRICE

Jay Weaver

GRETA GARBO, *Painted by Jay Weaver*

JULIA FAYE'S Spanish Shawl FR

In the peak acting years of Swanson, Garbo, Crawford and Dietrich, when a movie star was a Real Star who acted and dressed the part, they were an immense influence on fashion all over the world. Not only the clothes worn in their films but also their personal wardrobes, widely photographed for fan and fashion magazines, added to their legion of imitators. Every change of hairdo, shape of lips or eyebrows, silhouette of suit or shoe was copied and duplicated. Today the big influences on fashion are more likely to stem from current events or world news. For example, we owe the rage for fur hats and coats to Russia; the Nehru jacket, oriental fabrics and caftans to the Far East. Movie stars no longer wield the power of former decades, when anything worn by such pacesetters as Garbo, Crawford, Swanson, Dietrich, Constance Bennett, Norma Shearer, Claudette Colbert, Kay Francis and Dolores Del Rio created fashion and started vogues. Yet the costumes of a movie itself can have a strong influence. *Tom Jones* produced a million ruffled shirts for men and sparked a whole new men's fashion change. *Dr. Zhivago* is credited with starting the fur-trimmed maxicoat. *Isadora* revived a fad for the scarf-wrapped head and long trailing ends.

And what about the impact of *Bonnie and Clyde* and *Thoroughly Modern Millie?* The look of the 20s and 30s was suddenly revived on the very young everywhere as a result of these films. The current *The Damned* has continued the fashion influence of the 30s, when everything was pastel and the ladies loved mauve-beige, pistachio green and ivory.

In his book, *The Fashionable Savages,* John Fairchild, publisher of *Women's Wear Daily,* says that stars don't need fashion. Great stars forget fashion, dress for themselves and still set trends. Garbo, he says, is way above fashion, yet she still influences. Milliners continue to make her floppy slouch hat—the hat that is part of the fashion dictionary—"a Garbo."

Dietrich, he continues, is chic, well groomed, tailored and turned out in the tradition of Balenciaga, whom he calls the father of disciplined, understated clothes. Dietrich herself says, "He is the leader. I don't know any other Paris designer who knows so much about the actual making of clothes. . . . What is possible and what isn't . . . what cuts are correct for any given design. . . . The first fitting at Balenciaga is like the third fitting at any other house."

Luis Estevez picks Dietrich, Swanson and Garbo among the stars he admires, and says, "A star is someone who creates atmosphere around herself, a personal magnetism . . . someone who has glamour and talent. Garbo is one of the great glamour people of all time." Mme. Elsa Schiaparelli has dressed all Four Faces. I sat next to her at luncheon just recently and she told me about her clothes for all of them, and of a party she gave for Garbo in Paris. "I've known Gloria forever—started dressing her in the 20s." Norell dressed Swanson in *Zaza* and has turned out clothes for Crawford, Hepburn, Constance Bennett and Gertrude Lawrence.

Until the mid-20s, screen clothes bore little resemblance to those worn in real life. They were costumes that, as Howard Greer said, were somewhat of a marriage between the Schubert extravaganzas and Velázquez. Greer was one of the earliest designers to leave Broadway for Hollywood where he dressed Pola Negri, Evelyn Brent, Marion Davies, Norma Talmadge, Joan Crawford and Garbo.

Since the silent screen had no color or sound, it had to replace this loss with dramatic black and white dresses and costumes with plenty of contrast. As they were seen for only a few minutes, they were gaudy, exaggerated and overemphasized, but they did have imagination. A look at *Vogue* and *Harper's Bazaar* during that period shows that Parisian clothes were also pretty dramatic then. But as the influence of Chanel, Worth and Molyneux began to be felt, they became more simple; this fact was eventually reflected on the screen after stars like Swanson bought clothes in Paris and wore them in their films.

By the 30s, the screen clothes of Adrian, Travis Banton, Rene Hubert, Edith Head, Jean Louis, Orry Kelly, Irene, Eddie Stevenson and Greer were on a parallel with those of Paris in deciding the taste of women everywhere. By the mid-30s, it was these designers who set styles and started fads: they were unrivaled in their influence and inspiration. During the war, when Paris was sealed off, they were the sole influence. But their power waned with the decline of Hollywood. Some have died, and others retired, though a few like Jean Louis and Edith Head still do clothes for a few important stars and movies each year.

Still, for two decades the star syndrome and its celluloid queens set a pace never equaled before or since. The Greeks created a proverbial word for them: goddesses, which they were, indeed. With elegance and that extra dash of daring, the Stars made an art of presenting themselves, and no one has known anything like their fame and flair since then.

◀Swanson and designer Rene Hubert, who did her clothes for many years in such films as *The Trespasser, Music in the Air* and *Father Takes a Wife*.
[Oval] *What a Widow,* 1930. Gloria was among the very first to use leopard skin on hat and jacket.
▶Off-screen clothes, circa 1931.
A photograph taken while Swanson was living in Paris in 1957. She is one of "a distinguished jury of elegant Parisians, five American women and five French" for the *Réalités* Fashion Award. "Since they are the leaders of fashion, the dresses they choose will naturally prove to be the most successful, the most highly-prized, the most fashionable of the collection" *(Réalités,* November 1, 1957).
Left to right: Mme. Jean Masurel, Mme. Claude Serreulles, The Comtesse de Maud'huy, the Duchesse de Mouchy, the Duchess of Windsor, Mrs. Lauris Norstad, Gloria Swanson, Mrs. Charles Miller, Mme. Charles Saint and the Vicomtesse d'Harcourt.

She made the most of her lovely head with sleek hair and caps or closely molded toques.

◀ *Fine Manners*, 1926. Hat and dress trimmed with pheasant feathers in various colors.

▼ The flapper of *Zaza*, 1923.

▶ Off-screen hats in 1927 and 1928.

In spite of her small proportions, she could look regal in flowing draperies, arresting in unusual street clothes, and dashing in hats trimmed with feathers.

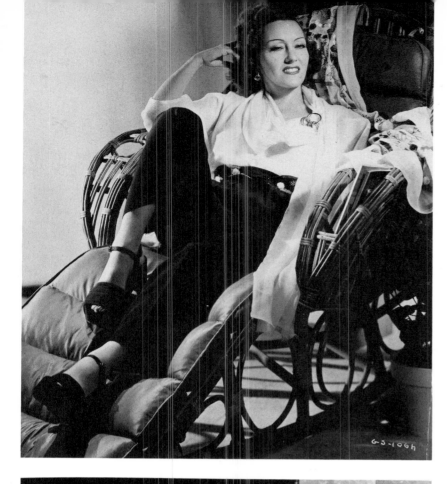

▲Gloria with Academy Award-winning designer Edith Head, at the time of *Sunset Boulevard.* Miss Head said of Gloria, "We are co-designers!"

Garbo *on screen* was memorable in
romantic, full-sleeved, off-the-shoulder
gowns and very contemporary with her
un-bra'd look in negligee pajamas with
long trousers that formed a train.
Adrian's cloche hat became a classic as
did his gowns, which showed the same
architectural simplicity as the hats.
Off screen, she preferred slacks,
sweaters, tweeds, low shoes and casual
coats.

Just say "Garbo" and her face comes to mind—the long neck, heavy-lidded eyes, thin brows and the long, soft hair. Also there is the memory of her in a snug beret, and a tilted Eugenie hat, both of which made one concentrate on her expressive face. They swept the fashion world in 1930.

THE KISS, 1929 ▼ *SUSAN LENNOX, 1931* ►
The clothes that Garbo wore were very advanced and
have a dateless quality. Although she was a tall, big
woman, she could look fragile and feminine.
Adrian said, "At first, they hung bangles and glass
beads on her. They considered her a sort of decorative
prop. I saw that she was like a tree with deep roots—
deep in the earth. You must never, never put an artificial
jewel or imitation lace on Garbo. Not that it would be
noticed on the screen, but it would do something to
Garbo and her performance."

◀Garbo in the swashbuckling clothes for *Queen Christina*, 1933, in which she wore leather jerkins, boots and plumed hats. Other memorable hats were the pillbox of *Grand Hotel*, 1932 *(above left)*, and a hat she herself designed for *Ninotchka*, 1939 (which is reminiscent of the Dietrich hat in *Angel*), *above right. Bottom right, The Painted Veil.*

In an article entitled "The Most Copied Girl in the World" in *Motion Picture* magazine, May 1937, Dorothy Spensley recalled Crawford's huge puffed sleeves, wide-lapeled polo coats, unplucked eyebrows, Zulu sun tan, square-shouldered suits and gowns, starched jabots, and huge hats, all inaugurated by Crawford. "From Boston to Budapest to Bali they copy the way she walks, the way she dresses, the way she does her hair—trains her brows—paints her lips."

Crawford said, "If I'm copied, it's because of my clothes and Adrian designs those. He is responsible for all of that." However, Adrian did not design the curve of her brow, the cut of her hair; nor did he decide that she was to abandon stockings, adopt sandals. He said, "Joan is a very definite and bold person. That's why she is copied. There is not a negative thing about her. So thousands of women are impelled to copy her, not only because they think they look like her, but because they hope they can achieve the positive quality that is her great attraction." The result was thousands of carbon-copy Crawfords—starting with the "wind-blown" look of *Our Dancing Daughters.* Copies of Crawford's costumes were in shop windows almost before her films were released. She was the progenitor of so many fashion trends and the perfect prototype of the movie star–fashion model.

MGMP-1147

Joan Crawford: "Our Dancing Daughter," "Letty Lynton" and, by the mid-30s, "the most copied girl in the world."

Left: With designer Paul Poiret and *(below right)* with Adrian.
Above: Two photographs from *Vogue* (February 1933), which said, "Here are more Hollywood originations that may influence the future: Joan Crawford's hat of woven grosgrain designed by Adrian—a hat taken up by that smart New Yorker, Mrs. Jules Glaenzer."

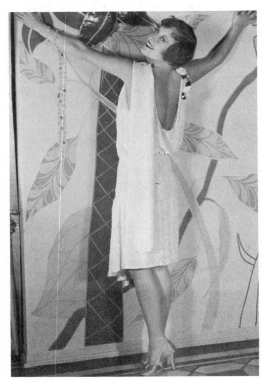

JOAN IN THE EARLY 30's.

THE MID AND LATE 30s.

THE 40s AND 50s.

Crawford's shoulders were enhanced and exaggerated by Adrian: he accentuated them until they became as imposing as her melon mouth. By the mid-40s, they were considered distinctive parts of American architecture, masterpieces of nature and art.

In the early 30s, Dietrich and Garbo were chief rivals in the World Eroticism Stakes. Both were star-goddesses who made a unique impact by uniting the two sides of their nature, the feminine and the masculine, in the polarity of their dress. On screen, they were usually gowned in the most feminine creations, but off screen they appeared in man-tailored slacks, simple suits, loose trench coats and mannish fedoras.

Dietrich is seen here with designer Travis Banton, the unsurpassed master of boudoir exotica.
▲ A wrap of cream-colored velvet, lavish with red-fox furs. The
sleeves have bell-shaped cuffs banded in fur, and the train of the
coat is bordered with fox.
▶ A minaret tunic of Persian brocade, a metal cloth in bronze,
gold and red tones, is worn with a slim skirt of midnight-
blue jersey.

Shanghai Express, her clothes were constructed right down to the
st feather, bead and sequin by director Josef Von Sternberg with
avis Banton, then bound together with eloquent camera angles and
ductive lighting that created black mystery. Banton continued dressing
r in feathers during the 30s, seducing the eyes with gorgeous glamour
wns that were form-fitting, elaborately decorated . . . all satin and
quins or feathers and chiffon. She was his favorite of all the stars he
essed, and his clothes for her were unsurpassed in memorable
vishness.

This layout is quite a contrast to the elaborately feminine clothes that preceded it. Here is the spectacular chic of white suits, beret, hats, and caps contrasting with the black velvet lounging suit by Jean Louis which seems so contemporary.

Edith Head said, "You don't design clothes for Dietrich, you design them with her."

◀ The black dress, slit to expose her beautiful legs, that won Dietrich a standing ovation on the Academy Award Show in 1949. A few years ago while in Dallas for a performance, Dietrich went shopping at Neiman-Marcus outfitted in custom-made bluejeans, Western jacket, boots and cowboy hat. As she left the store where she had attracted a great deal of attention, a tall Texan, clad in business suit, cowboy boots and hat, stepped up to her and asked in a Western drawl, "Pardon me, Ma'am, but aren't you Marlene Dietrich?"

She gave him a slow take, eyed him up and down from boots to Stetson, then gave her own cowboy hat a more rakish tilt with a gesture that was a kind of salute and replied, "Yup."

X

MASTERS OF THE CAMERA

This is a chapter of famous portraits by some of the master photographers of the 20th century. Their judgment, discernment and authority have immeasurably contributed to the history and changing whims of Beauty, Glamour and Style during the past fifty years. Their critical taste, analytical eyes and sovereignty over the camera have made them true arbiters of what has been "new," what has been chic, what has been desirable. Through their insight and technique, they have, time and time again, expertly and eloquently shown the amazing versatility of the human face.

Here are Gloria Swanson, Greta Garbo, Joan Crawford, and Marlene Dietrich seen through the eyes of these internationally renowned photographers, in portraits that range from the carefully planned and posed to the casually improvised and unrehearsed. Here is an infinite variety of images and moods that are tranquil, happy, sad and exuberant, captured in magical moments to add to this definitive study of Four Fabulous Faces. It is an inimitable and striking ensemble of portraits—a timeless gallery of Beauty—which begins with two Maurice Goldberg portraits of Gloria Swanson taken in 1925. The one on the left would seem to be inspired by Max Reinhardt's play, *The Miracle,* an elaborately staged import from Germany that was something of a sensation during the 1924–25 Broadway season. Note the stigma on Swanson's hand.

There is an interesting history to the Arnold Genthe portraits of Garbo on page 456. In 1925, when director Maurice Stiller brought Garbo to America, they spent several lonely, unhappy months during the summer in New York City where they found the heat unbearably oppressive and the reluctance of the M-G-M executives to send them to the West Coast both puzzling and frightening. Hoping to whet the studio's interest, Stiller arranged a screen test for Garbo, but the Metro officials found her "too unusual" and indicated that there were few roles for her type. Discouraged, the director and his find were considering a return to Sweden when an actress-friend of Stiller's (Martha Hedman) took them to the studio of an important photographer, Arnold Genthe. They spoke in German and, as she relaxed, Garbo said that she'd love to be photographed some time by him. "Why not now?" he asked. So the famous portraits shown on page 456 were made without any further preparation. Throwing a few yards of cloth over her dress, he captured such distinctive poses and expressions that it was hard to believe they were of the same girl. All were delighted with the results.

Later, Garbo came to the studio to thank him and to say goodbye. "They don't seem to want me... I'm going back to Berlin." Genthe asked her to show his pictures to the people at Metro. (Meanwhile he sent copies to *Vanity Fair*, which published one in its November issue, captioned, "A New Star from the North—Greta Garbo.") When the studio officials saw the oddly provocative face that Genthe had captured, they agreed that maybe she *could* have a future with them. So another contract was drawn up, and finally she and Stiller left for Hollywood. Thus, by the strange quirk of a casual evening of unplanned photographs, one of the greatest faces of all time had her career saved.

The Cecil Beaton portraits of Garbo on pages 462 and 463, in gay, exuberant moods, look remarkably like the young Garbo of the 20s, when her hair was darker, her teeth uncapped and her eyebrows natural and unplucked.

MAURICE GOLDBERG, 1925.

MAURICE GOLDBERG, 1925.

MARCUS BLECHMAN, 1955.

DOROTHY WILDING, 1933.

446

GEORGE PLATT LYNES, 1941.

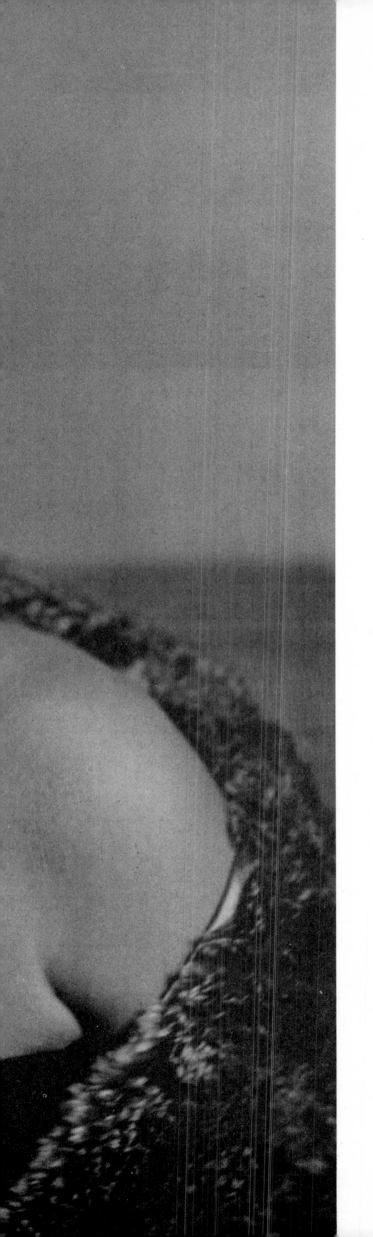

CLIFFORD COFFIN, 1950.

RICHARD AVEDON, 1950.

EDWARD CARROLL, 1966.

ARNOLD GENTHE. 1925.

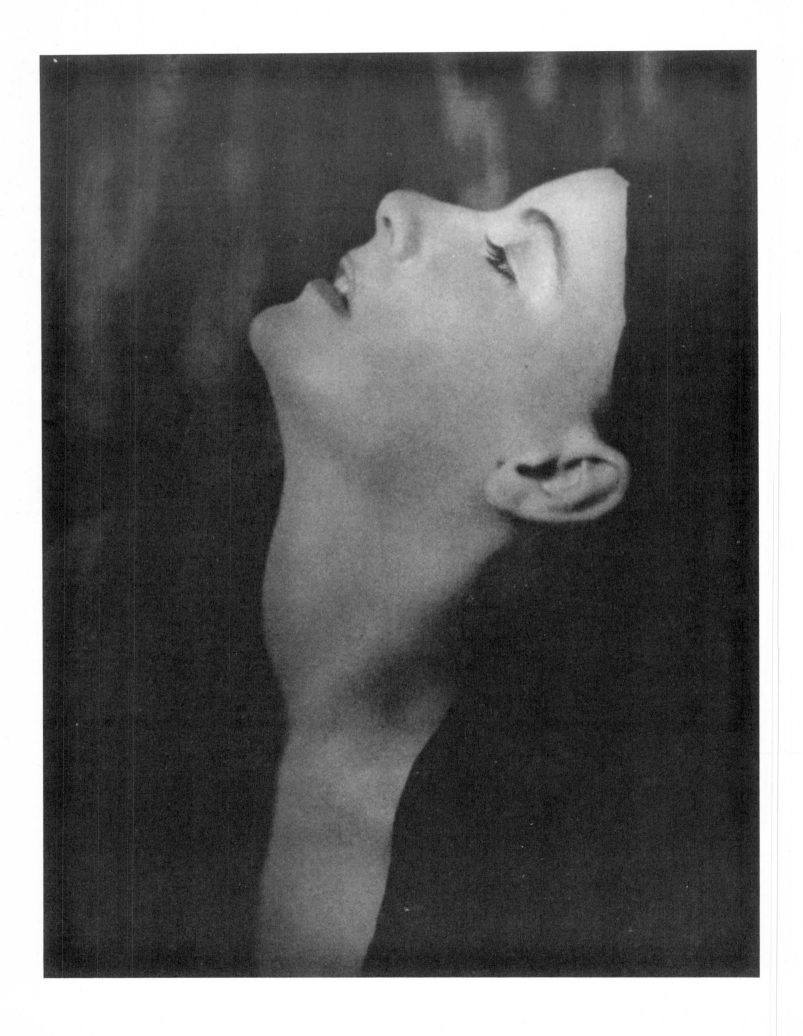

ARNOLD GENTHE, 1925.

ANTHONY BEAUCHAMP, circa 1955.

CECIL BEATON, mid-50's and mid-60's.

CECIL BEATON, 1931

MORTIMER OFFNER, 1930

HORST B. HORST, 1940

CECIL BEATON, 1956

GEORGE PLATT LYNES

468

ANTON BRUEL, 1936

HORST P. HORST, 1948

RICHARD AVEDON, 1948

476

IRVING PENN, 1948

JOHN RAWLINGS, 1941

MILTON GREENE, 1952

XI

THE RECENT YEARS

"What are they doing now?" is a question that continues to interest many people and one that obviously should interest anyone who has read through this book to these final pages. The other question that inevitably is asked is, "What is her *real* age?" a subject I've purposely avoided discussing until this chapter. Since the two queries are related, let's take a look at the four subjects as of today (1970).

From the best authenticated records, Gloria Swanson was born March 27, 1899, Marlene Dietrich on December 27, 1901, Joan Crawford on March 23, 1904, and Greta Garbo on September 18, 1905. So they were born within a period of six and a half years, contemporaries in age as well as careers. To me, the point of their age is of interest primarily because, to their everlasting credit, they still are able to look as they do and because they remain such remarkably active and interesting women. For the most part, each follows the pattern of living she set up for herself many years ago. The habits that were developed during the peak years of performing still persist now, even though the acting career, itself, is no longer paramount.

It should be pointed out that the photographs in this chapter, in contrast to those seen in previous portions of the book, are all candid and un-retouched. They are not "glamour photographs," carefully lighted and posed to flatter the subjects. But their very honesty and candor show the character and strength of the four—the essence of their personalities. (Certainly, we all know what a candid snapshot taken at any age can look like; sometimes they can be very unflattering. Needless to say, that is not the intention here.)

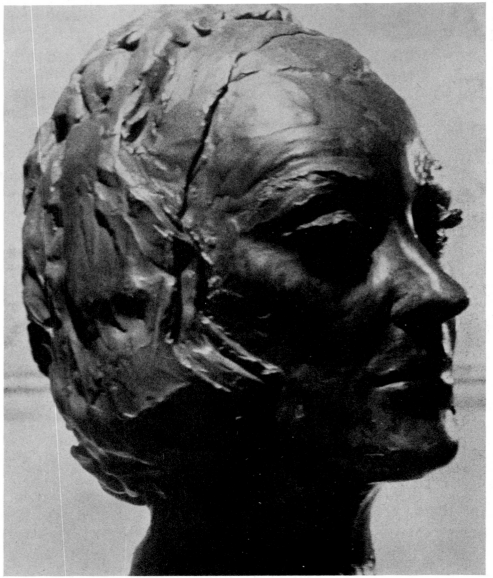

A sculpted head which she did of herself recalls that Swanson was nominated by that *arbiter elegantiarum* of magazines, *Vanity Fair*, for its Hall of Fame in September, 1924, "because she is a sculptress, writer, linguist and musician of first rate ability . . . and because her sure and restrained acting have made her a noted screen artist." Multitalented, magnetic and mercurial, she designs clothes, paints portraits, promotes her own line of cosmetics, health foods and a salad dressing, her activities fed and generated by the current of her prodigious will.

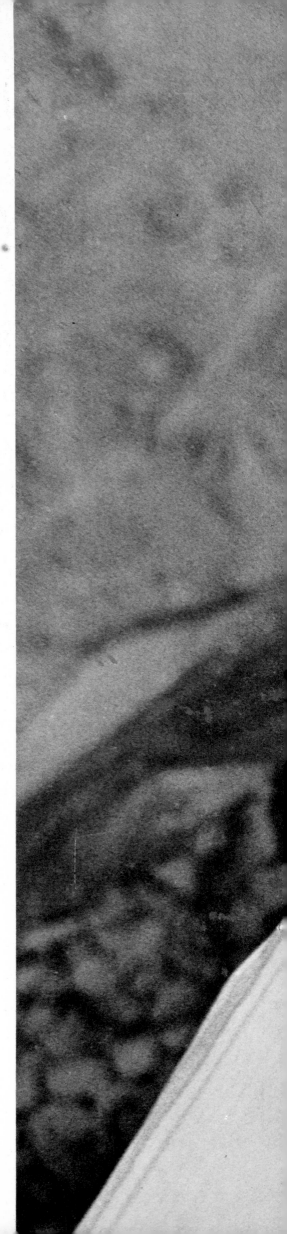

For over fifty years now, Gloria Swanson has been a star whose beauty has had a lasting, unique appeal to both men and women. Her dazzling vitality, her deep interest in everything that goes on in the world continue unabated. Her daily schedule often wears out people half her age.

She lectures on health, food, and diet; has a fashion line of clothes, and has a recent line of Gloria Swanson cosmetics (which "are so pure they're edible. Have some," invites Gloria). Congressman James J. Delancey, in the October 22, 1969, issue of the *New York Times,* credits Swanson for being partially responsible for an amendment that barred the artificial sweetener, cyclamate, from diet food and drinks. "Miss Swanson had quite a grasp of the subject and when she got before the Congressmen's wives, she was quite a spellbinder," he said.

Her professional career during the past decade has included acting chores on several TV series: "Dr. Kildare," "The Beverly Hillbillies," "Straightaway," "Alfred Hitchcock Presents," "Burke's Law," etc. She has been a frequent, articulate guest on the talk shows of Jack Paar, Johnny Carson, David Frost, Mike Douglas, Joey Bishop, Art Linkletter and Steve Allen. Audiences have seen her "in person" in such plays as *Reprise, Inkwell, Between Seasons, The Women, Let Us Be Gay* and *Reflected Glory.* (Earlier, Gloria appeared on Broadway, starring in *A Goose for the Gander, 20th Century* and *Nina.*) In December, 1968 she went to Russia on a one-woman unofficial cultural exchange tour to promote the two greatest interests of her life, health foods and movies. While there, she was invited by the Soviet film industry in Moscow to hostess a screening of *Sunset Boulevard,* that dark valentine about the Hollywood of old. At the conclusion of the film, the members of the Russian film industry gave her a standing ovation for the performance in a film made nearly twenty years earlier.

Swanson, once a Marquise and always a queen, with her neon-flashing smile and ageless sex appeal, continues to be a Living Legend—a Fabulous Face.

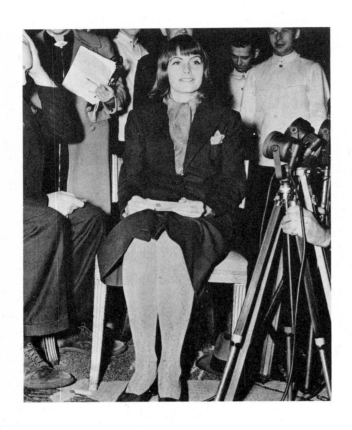

Garbo's life today seems a lonely one without purpose or direction. Like many people who live alone, as she grows older, she has become more set in her ways, more self-centered, more demanding. She has hinted that she wants to appear on the stage again and talks of acting in another film. But she needs a strong personality—someone dominant and decisive—to organize any such projects since she, herself, has neither the know-how nor the courage to accomplish it. With no real goals, she walks the streets of the world searching for something she never finds, interested, only momentarily, by whatever may distract her. Now in her middle sixties, she has a limited group of friends with whom she can share her activities. There is no family, no husband or ex-husband, no children, no relatives and the dwindling coterie of friends and admirers gets fewer each year. Some die away and others become disenchanted and less inclined to pay the high price that Garbo demands for friendship which is *everything* on *her* terms.

Yet, when the mood strikes her, she can be very gay and the most engaging of companions. And because these moods are so rare, her friends consider them very precious and feel gratified to be able to share them. She has a dry, wry wit that can be quite devastating on the one hand and a child-like sense of humor and laughter that is very endearing on the other.

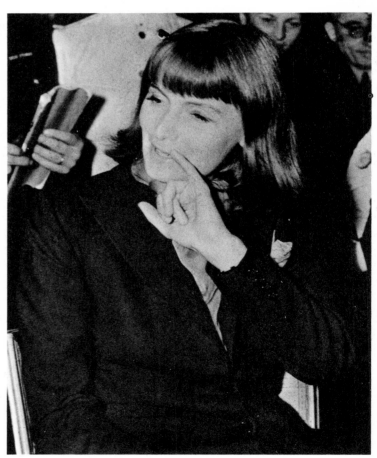

During her career and ever since her retirement, Garbo has been pursued by throngs of eager, aggressive reporters and news photographers. Any trip sets up this hectic pursuit of her, but only on rare occasions has she consented to pose for her pursuers. On page 484 are some informal shots taken aboard the *Kungsholm,* 1938, on a return visit to Sweden, one of the few times that she submitted to the ordeal of a press conference.

She will usually go to any lengths to avoid reporters: this behavior pattern was begun during her alliance with Maurice Stiller and she has continued it ever since. In the Hollywood days, one reporter who had shadowed her for weeks finally came face to face with her; it's a toss-up as to who was the more startled. He was rewarded for his patience with an explosive "Damn" from Garbo and the incident became known as the famous one-word interview.

As she grows older, more rigid, more spoiled, she has become almost neurotic in her attempts to avoid confrontation with the press and her public as she continues her lonely existence, wandering the world and fleeing from all who recognize her.

Left: A candid shot taken in 1949 on the *Ile de France.*
Lower right: Another boat trip in the 50s.

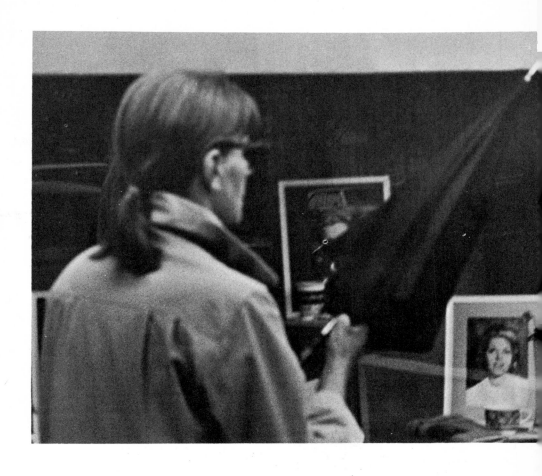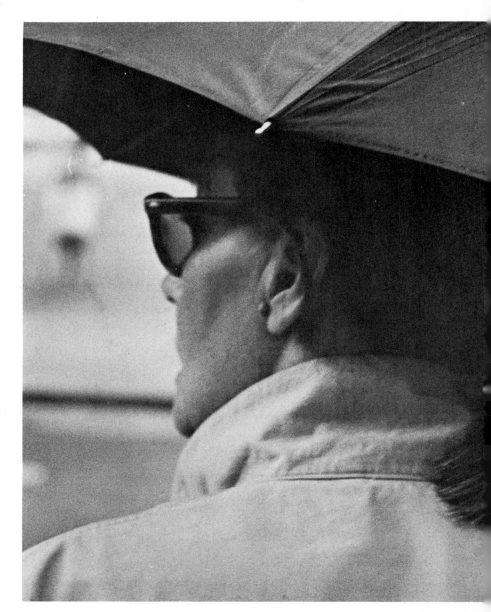

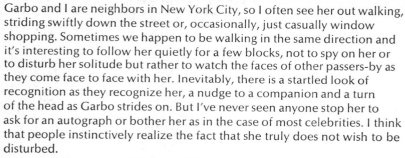

Garbo and I are neighbors in New York City, so I often see her out walking, striding swiftly down the street or, occasionally, just casually window shopping. Sometimes we happen to be walking in the same direction and it's interesting to follow her quietly for a few blocks, not to spy on her or to disturb her solitude but rather to watch the faces of other passers-by as they come face to face with her. Inevitably, there is a startled look of recognition as they recognize her, a nudge to a companion and a turn of the head as Garbo strides on. But I've never seen anyone stop her to ask for an autograph or bother her as in the case of most celebrities. I think that people instinctively realize the fact that she truly does not wish to be disturbed.

Recently when I was waiting for a friend in front of her apartment (she and Garbo live on the same block), I was talking to the doorman when Garbo passed by. He observed, "Miss Garbo is sure some walker." I asked, "Do you see her often?" and he replied, "Every day when she's in town. I've watched her for twenty years and she's always out walking, no matter what the weather is. It would wear me out—but she's a very fine lady" he concluded as my friend came out. She and I walked down the street behind Garbo watching with interest the faces of other pedestrians as she passed them. She walks quickly, usually glancing neither left nor right until something in a shop window catches her eye. She will stop for a moment to window shop until she becomes aware that she is being watched then she will continue on.

A well-known stage director who lives in the same building as I told me of going to an appointment one day and becoming aware that Garbo was walking alongside him. Both were stopped by the same traffic lights at several corners and silently observed one another. They continued in the same direction until he came to the building where his appointment was. He said that he was there for several hours and when he left to walk back home it was quite late in the afternoon. Stopping at the first traffic light, he was startled to find Garbo again standing next to him. They glanced at each other and, in mock severity, he inquired, "Are you following me?" She roared with laughter, took his arm and said, "Come, walk me home." He reported that they had a delightful, relaxed walk, talking casual chitchat as one does with a neighbor. He refers to the incident as "the day Garbo picked me up."

112

She has made an institution of herself—a firm—
an organization—one who observes no union hours
but works round the clock selling that trade-
marked intangible, herself. Her memory is
phenomenal! With the practical skill of a veteran
politician, she can remember first names after a
single meeting. This has been a tremendous asset
socially and with her fans (she greets them by
name on the street and chats with them as bosom
pals, asking about their personal lives with
affection), in her film work and in her hard-
driving promotional work for Pepsi-Cola.

Thriving on her success and the accompanying
adulation, she instantly becomes the center of
attraction in any gathering. She is a great star
who acts like a star, talks like a star and displays
herself as a star, always impeccably groomed and
dressed to the teeth.

It's impossible for her to break the habits developed by forty-five years of making films. She is
an actress to the core, with authority and a
complete knowledge of lights, stories, direction,
pace; one who is fanatically punctual for any
appointment. When people talk about her, they
invariably use words like ''discipline,'' ''ageless,''
''indomitable'' and ''durable.'' In forty-five
years, she has truly earned these accolades. I
suppose that she and Garbo and Swanson and
Dietrich will always be around. I hope so!

In the early 1950's Dietrich starred in a half-hour Sunday radio series entitled "Cafe Istanbul." As Mademoiselle Madou, Dietrich was owner-entertainer of the intrigue-filled cafe. While each episode was complete in itself, the series had many of the same characters appearing weekly and the scriptwriters—undoubtedly knowingly—gave most of Dietrich's gentlemen friends names that contained an *r* sound: Chris (which the lady of course pronounced Cwis) and Raoul (Wawoul). Toward the close of one of the week's installments, Dietrich promised to meet

"Cwis" on the "woof" but, angry at him, never kept her promise. During the week following that particular episode, Miss Dietrich attended Betty Hutton's opening at the Palace. (In true Palace tradition Miss Hutton opened at the matinee, but Dietrich and the other celebrities went to the first Saturday evening performance.) At intermission, a fan, spotting the object of his affection, approached Dietrich and requested an autograph. Nodding and with a great flourish, she scrawled an oversized "Dietrich" across the program photo of Miss Hutton. As she returned his program the fan said, "Miss Dietrich, you should never have left Chris waiting on the roof." Miss Dietrich observed her admirer without cracking a smile and, still holding his pen, replied, "Oh? Shouldn't I have?" The fan flushed and said, "No." Miss Dietrich, never losing her cool and always in character, turned to go. As she did, she peered over her shoulder and said, "Don't worry. He'll come back." She walked away, took about five steps, turned around again and said, "They always come back."
(In *The Blue Angel,* she had said: "You'll come back—they always do!")